# Community of Faith

# COMMUNITY OF FAITH ✤

Models and Strategies for Developing
Christian Communities

EVELYN EATON WHITEHEAD
and JAMES D. WHITEHEAD

The Winston • Seabury Press

Grateful acknowledgment is made for permission to use materials by Evelyn Eaton
Whitehead which appeared originally in the following sources:
"Clarifying the Meaning of Community" in *The Living Light* 15 (1978):376-92.
"Ministers Need Three Communities" in *National Catholic Reporter,* July 18, 1978, p. 8.
Parts of "The Structure of Community" from *The Parish in Community and Ministry*
(Paulist Press, 1978), pp. 35-52.

Library of Congress Catalog Card Number: 81-18411
ISBN: 0-86683-949-6 (previously ISBN: 0-8164-2370-9)

Printed in the United States of America
5    4    3    2    1

The Winston • Seabury Press
430 Oak Grove
Minnepolis, Minnesota 55403

*for*
Mary and Gene Ulrich,
Ivan and Megan and Laura

*where community begins*

# Contents

# Introduction

Christianity is a community event. As Christians we have always believed that the life of faith is not a private enterprise but a communal venture. Over the past several decades in the Church we have come to renewed awareness of this fact. One of the most significant efforts within the Church today is the movement of Christians to understand themselves as the people of God and to experience their relations with one another as a life together in community. We rejoice in this vision of Christian life, taking hope in its challenge to the formality and bureaucracy that can find their way into church structures. But, gradually, many of us have come to sense that this goal of life together as Christians is both a gift and a most difficult ambition.

The language of ministry today is filled with the vocabulary of mutuality: mutual support, shared decision-making, collegiality, and collaboration. These ideals have generated a renewed commitment to the ministry of community formation. But for some of us these ideals have become stumbling blocks. Having given ourselves generously to the effort of community formation, we come away with a sense of frustration, failure, and confusion. Team ministry is more difficult than we imagined it would be; parish councils have not lived up to our expectations; shared decision-making has been, in practice, a rare phenomenon. Confronted with this gap between our religious rhetoric and our practical experience, we are forced to reexamine our expectations of Christian community.

In the chapters which follow we take up this effort of reexamination. This book is not an attempt to deny the experience of discouragement and confusion regarding religious efforts toward community. Its goal is to contribute to the possibility of community in the Church today through an effort of clarification. Within sociology and psychology a consensus is emerging concerning the characteristics of community as a style of group life. Few nonspecialists have access to this information. The language of the social sciences remains foreign to many, even to those well-educated and well-read in other areas of contemporary culture. The intent of this volume is to provide access—to make more directly available to the adult believer and to the reflective minister the resources of the social sciences on the question of community. The discussion which follows can be understood as an attempt to "befriend" the social sciences so that their power may be put at the service of the mission and ministry of the Christian people. Befriending will involve some acquaintance with the perspective from which sociologists and psychologists view the question of community and with their findings regarding group life. Befriending will also include a critical awareness of the limits of the social sciences. Sociology alone will not resolve the dilemmas of Christian community, but it can make an important contribution. Its perspective can be especially useful in helping us to clarify issues and elements that are a part of the ongoing experience of life together.

For a full and fruitful exploration of the possibilities of Christian community today, the resources of the social sciences must be set in assertive dialogue with people's actual experience of life together and with religious images and ideals of community. It is conversation among these three authoritative sources—personal experience, Christian tradition, and contemporary social sciences—that can best contribute to the building up of the community of faith. This volume attempts to contribute to this conversation.

The method of this reflection on Christian community follows what we have described in our book *Method in Ministry*. The resources of the social sciences are brought into dialogue here with the images and ideals of community life that we share as Christians. We invite readers to bring to this reflection their own experiences of community living. Reflective exercises at the end of each chapter are provided to help identify these experiences—positive and negative—and to help clarify the convictions that accompany them.

A ministry of community formation must begin in a ministry of clarification: What are our expectations of the parish or religious congregation today? What are the cultural forces that undercut or inhibit our religious ambition for a shared life of faith? In the following chapters we will explore some of the stresses and possibilities in contemporary Christian communities. The discussion of the social structure of community (Part II) and the psychological dynamics of life together (Part IV) is supported by theological reflection on the pluralistic nature of the community of faith today (Part I), the community as nurturer of personal and collective dreams (Part III), and the "sense of the faithful" at the core of the community's life of faith (Part V). As we offer our own considerations on the multifaceted question of community, we are aware of the valuable work being done by many others. It has not been our intent to fully survey or report this wealth. We do, however, offer at the end of each chapter a selection of additional resources that readers may find useful. For those interested in pursuing further the social sciences' analysis of community, the Appendix provides an overview of this area and a listing of additional resources which may serve as an initial guide.

This book is intended for use among a wide range of groups in the Church who struggle to understand themselves as community. These include parishes, ministry teams, religious congregations, local religious houses, parish councils and committees, school faculties, prayer groups, support groups, religious education networks, task force groups, and religious movements for political action. Many (though certainly not all) groups in each of these categories see the religious ideal of community as a model of their life together and as a goal of their interaction. This book will assist these groups to understand the issues that give shape to group life. It will also suggest the shape of an effective ministry of community formation.

As we turn to our discussion of community, we are pleased to acknowledge the contribution that has been made by others, particularly our colleagues at the Institute of Pastoral Studies at Loyola University in Chicago. In the courses we have taught with them, G. V. Egan and J. Gordon Myers have broadened our perspective on the issues involved in community formation. Early on, Patricia

McCarthy, William G. Thompson, and Joan Scanlon encouraged us to continue in the direction of our own analysis by sharing with us their sense of its value to the discussions of community life in religious congregations today. James Zullo and Lucien Roy offered support by word and by deed, making use of some of our materials in their own work and, in the process, improving them. We are especially grateful to our friend Michael Cowan for letting us include here material from his ongoing analysis of community life.

For all that the Institute of Pastoral Studies has contributed over the past decade to our own work—and, more significantly, to the life of the American Church—credit goes preeminently to Jerome A. O'Leary. Director of the Institute from 1970 through June of 1982, Jerry has stimulated a network of intellectual competence and pastoral creativity there that has nurtured many. With them, we salute his leadership and offer our thanks.

# ✤ PART I

## UNDERSTANDING THE COMMUNITY OF FAITH

# 1

# Pluralism and the Christian Community

## The Rhetoric and the Experience of Community

The contemporary crisis in Christian community—how we are to live together, believe together, and support each other through our unbelief—centers, in part, on the widening gap between our rhetoric and our experience of life together. In religious life and education, rhetoric plays an important role in calling us to our best hopes and ideals. A gap necessarily exists between rhetoric and experience, reminding us of the personal and corporate change that our ideals demand. Religious rhetoric shapes our expectations; it "images" a better, holier way to live. When these expectations become too removed from our experience, a crisis ensues.

Community life is always about unity and pluralism: in a parish or religious congregation or other form of community, we attempt to bring diverse lives and experiences into one. Religious rhetoric in the Christian tradition has always embraced both themes of unity and pluralism. The Church is both one and catholic; as catholic it embraces and unifies a wide diversity of believers. But since this diversity so often appears as a threat to our unity, the rhetoric of our tradition has especially stressed the theme of unity. In the gospels we find Jesus praying to his Father that "They may be one, even as we are one" (Jn. 17:22). This intimate unity has always been seen as a goal of Christian life together. Perhaps the most powerful image of the believing community has been that of a single body. (See Rom. 12, 1 Cor. 12, and Eph. 4.) The aptness of this image is its combination of singleness and pluralism. At periods in the Church we have been much more intent on the oneness of this body than on the necessary diversity and even conflict among its plural members.

In recent Roman Catholic history for instance the rhetoric of unity concerning the believing community has led to powerful expectations of uniformity. Catholics celebrated Mass in the same way, in the same language, throughout the world; Catholic spirituality developed in uniform practices—meatless Fridays, the rosary, Stations of the Cross; Catholics knew what they believed on every moral question. Such an emphatic celebration of unity and uniformity, with all the powerful and positive bonding that it achieved, did have a significant price: it entailed forgetting the ministerial and liturgical variety that existed in other rites (married priests; different languages used in the Eucharist), and necessitated a denial of Protestant life as genuinely Christian.

Most recently this rhetoric of intense unity has been challenged by profound experiences of diversity. Parishes today confront an enormous divergence in needs and expectations among their members: some Catholics are content to have the community function as a cultural context for weddings and other human passages, while other believers look for opportunities for intense small-group faith sharing. In many large parishes Catholics hear homilies about Christian intimacy and fellowship, but they experience the parish, with its extended physical plant, as a part of an international institution. Another area of diversity has appeared as more Catholics today want to participate in the Church's ministry, a ministry once stably and ably manned by male, celibate priests. More threatening yet, Catholics even seem at odds among themselves in their beliefs about such central issues as sexuality or justice or religious authority. The uniformity of our Catholic life-style is eroding and we urgently need ways to understand what seems to be a new and rampant religious diversity within Catholic life.

The challenge has to do with the nature of religious change.[1] Can

1. Church historian Jaroslav Pelikan discusses "the incapacity of classical Christian thought to come to terms with change" in his "Theology and Change," *Cross Currents* (Fall 1969), p. 375. The effort to find an unchanging core of dogma in the midst of what was and is, in fact, a pluriformity of belief and practice is given excellent treatment by Robert Wilken in his *The Myth of Christian Beginnings*, (Notre Dame, IN: University of Notre Dame Press, 1980). See pp. 184–185 for a summary statement of the extraordinary pluralism which constitutes the Christian faith. Catholic theologians have struggled with this question of change in terms of the development of dogma—how a revelation seemingly given in its fullness in Jesus Christ unfolds, finding significantly different interpretation over time. Raymond Brown reviews the crisis-inducing changes in Catholic understandings of scripture in Chapter One of *Crises Facing the Church* (New York: Paulist Press, 1975).

the religious pluralism we are experiencing in our life together have some positive value? Can it be interpreted as more than scandal, more than merely a result of sin and human failure? In the following pages we will discuss the experience of pluralism in two significant areas of Christian community: (1) an emerging pluralism in Catholic ministry and (2) pluralism in faith itself. Before exploring these areas, it will be useful to reflect on pluralism in the Christian tradition and on three possible interpretations of religious diversity.

## Pluralism and the Christian Tradition

The one faith that Christians confess has from the beginning of our history been believed and expressed plurally. This was necessarily the case for a faith that was intended for all nations (Mt. 28:19): as a universal religion, not limited to a single culture or race, Christianity would necessarily find plural expression on different continents and in diverse cultural contexts. Also, as a faith which confessed God's presence throughout history and not just in a single, privileged moment of revelation, Christianity was committed to continually attending to God's voice in human history. Such plural attending would mean differing interpretations of this mysterious presence.

But the pluralism of Christianity is not merely a result of this faith's spread through different nations and over changing centuries. This pluralism and diversity in belief and conviction existed from the very outset. Peter and Paul had very different notions about Christian observance of Jewish law. In the first generations of Christianity communities differed in their religious response to Christ.[2] The scriptures themselves present strikingly divergent interpretations of the end-time and the return of Jesus. Paul's writings reveal a changing understanding of the nearness of this end-time and God's final judgment. Whereas the synoptic gospels witness to an end-time that is to come, the fourth gospel displays a realized eschatology: "He who hears my word and believes him

2. William Thompson examines Peter and Paul's differences in "Conflict, Anger and Growth in the Church," *Chicago Studies*, 12 (1973): 39–46. He argues for the potential usefulness of conflict in the growth of a pluralistic Church. On the differing Christologies in Antioch and Corinth, see Helmut Koester's "Gnomai Diaphoroi: The Origin and Nature of Diversification in the History of Early Christianity," *Harvard Theological Review*, 58 (1965): 279–318. On diversity within the Johannine community itself see Raymond Brown's " 'Other Sheep in the Fold': The Johannine Perspective on Christian Diversity in the Late First Century," *Journal of Biblical Literature*, 97 (1978): 5–22.

who sent me, has eternal life; he does not come into judgment, but has already passed from death to life" (Jn. 5:24). The paradox of God's kingdom as both to come and already alive in us demands plural formulations. The scriptures and the witness of the earliest Christian communities do not, then, present a picture of uniform belief; they are not, in fact, *una voce dicentes*. If our own acute experience of religious pluralism has made us more aware of the pluralism in early Christianity, we are still faced with the evaluation of such diversity. Three quite different interpretations seem possible; pluralism as scandal; pluralism as relativism; or pluralism as a sign of richness.

### Pluralism as Scandal

Religious diversity can be and often is seen simply as scandal. Differing views and expressions of belief appear to be regrettable and should be reduced to a single, true understanding of the Christian faith. Here pluriformity stands as a sign of disunity, division, and, perhaps, disloyalty. Variety is seen as divergence from a single, stable norm and represents varieties of unbelief and false belief rather than a variety of belief. Much of the diversity in Christian life may, indeed, be a result of sin and willful antagonisms, but if *all* diversity is suspect, then this bias that sees pluralism as scandal is in evidence.

This hostile interpretation seems often to be rooted in a fundamentalist view of reality and faith. Everything (a person, an act, or a belief) has one stable identity and meaning. Each credal statement, such as "Jesus is the Christ," is understood to possess a single, unambiguous and unchanging meaning. About this and every aspect of Christian faith, there exists one right understanding and other, perhaps several, wrong understandings. A person either believes correctly or does not. A clear dualism of right and wrong, orthodox and heterodox, defines religous life. In such a context pluralism represents a (often willful, therefore, sinful) confusion of essentially clear realities.

At times, of course, pluralism may represent willful divergence in belief and expression, dictated more by mutual antagonism than by the complexity of reality. In its extreme, however, this position becomes a bias. Diversity is understood as essentially and always a scandal, one which results simply from a failure of vision or will.

## Pluralism as Relativism

At the other end of the continuum from an *a priori* rejection of pluralism is a full surrender to it. Here pluralism is most accurately described as a relativism: "people are just different" and "different religions are just different ways of seeking the same God." Such relativism may be an attempt to avoid the conflicts and confusion which arise when we take seriously the diversity of our beliefs. In the religious arena, relativism functions as a theological "I'm OK; you're OK." Here pluralism is neither denied nor fully confronted; a religious privatism often results, in which individuals believe according to their own lights while trying not to disturb one another. The fundamentalist desire for clarity and uniformity is here replaced by a desire to avoid conflict. This bias toward relativism retreats even from the dialogue and healthy confrontation necessary to sustain an adult community of faith.

## Pluralism as a Sign of Richness

This view of pluralism attempts to steer between a rejection of and a surrender to human and religious diversity. It begins in a realization that pluralism is a characteristic of group life, and, in fact, a potential resource and sign of richness in communal life. Such a view, when understood as a theological position, is grounded in the conviction that we cannot, finally and clearly, comprehend God. Pluralism of belief and expression in this context points to the variegated and rich contributions to a single faith of its members' different beliefs.

Two examples of pluralistic belief will illustrate this attitude toward religious diversity. Christians all confess "Jesus is the Christ." This, in fact, defines a Christian: one who believes we are saved through the redemptive action of this man who is God. Yet, how do we adequately say this mystery of God-among-us? The gospel accounts themselves differ considerably in their presentation of this person. In Luke we meet a very human Jesus. In the fourth gospel, Jesus is portrayed as personified wisdom, the divine Word among us. The history of Christian piety and theology since these first generations of believers represents our efforts to say, re-say and say yet again what this mystery means to us. There are indeed boundaries to these sayings: to confess that God did not become flesh but appeared on earth in the guise of a human person is to cross over the boundary of orthodox Christian faith; at the other extreme, to assert that Jesus was only an extraordinarily holy human being is to also depart from Christian orthodoxy. But within these boundaries of orthodoxy, a wide variety of beliefs about Jesus as the Christ has flourished—from Christologies that present Jesus as omniscient in his mother's womb to Christologies in which this unique son of God grew gradually into his vocation and mission, sharing in the human process of growth through doubt and confusion. A fundamentalist will insist that only one of these differing Christologies can be right; a relativist might welcome not only these orthodox positions, but any pious effort to understand Jesus Christ. The third view of religious pluralism points to the ultimate ineffability of this mystery, not as simply counseling silence (a possible and logical consequence but one that most believers, especially theologians, have not been inclined to), but also as necessitating a pluralism of expression. By speaking plurally (as well as carefully) about this mystery we more richly confess what we do not fully understand. And this plural testimony is an act of a believing community; it is precisely the function of a community—be it a parish or the universal Church—to elicit, evaluate, and celebrate the variety of its orthodox beliefs about Jesus Christ.

A second example concerns how best to celebrate God's presence in the community. Instructed to enact the Eucharist in memory of Christ, we have done so under the motifs of both sacrifice and meal. "Which is right?" the fundamentalist would be first to ask. A response drawn from this third view of pluralism would be a zen-like "yes."

Generations of American Catholics have grown up with one style of liturgical celebration. In the liturgical reforms of the 1960s this uniformity was traded for a variety of styles of celebrations, in different languages, at different times. Some of these new styles of celebration are immature, as surely as an immature, unthinking participation was possible in an earlier, more uniform liturgy. This third view of religious pluralism points to the diversity of celebration as a potential resource of a community: different stages of belief and the desire for different degrees of participation are best responded to in differing liturgies.

The richness of Christian history is precisely its pluralistic efforts to understand and worship the Lord, both in formal theological reflection and liturgical expression. Instead of holding rigidly to one, unchangeable meaning of "Jesus is the Christ," or a single, inflexible mode of eucharistic celebration, we have continually explored new styles of belief and expression. The challenge has always been to frame this newness in a manner faithful both to the Christian tradition and to God's presence discerned in contemporary life.

Again this plural expression of belief is a function of a community. In community we find our individual biases and convictions bounded by, complemented by, and challenged by others. This is both a threat and a gift. As a gift my community—indeed my religious tradition—fills out the narrowness of my own vision, welcomes my strengths and special insights, and makes up for my limitations. Pluralism, in this understanding, is an essential characteristic of a believing community, not to be apologized for, denied, or simply overcome, but to be invoked as a resource and strength. This is *how* faith flourishes in a group and carries individual belief beyond itself; this is how we are incorporated and our faith made communal. Employing this third understanding of diversity we will now review two areas of religious pluralism which demand interpretation today.

### An Emerging Pluralism in Ministry

The earliest Christian communities seemed to have known a variety of ministries. St. Paul wrote of ministries of teaching, prophecy, healing, and administration (see 1 Cor. 12 for his mention of these and other ministries). These ministries arose out of "the varieties of gifts" distributed throughout the community by the Spirit. This variegation of ministries, which appears in Paul's letters as unhierarchized and only loosely coordinated, evolved over the first centuries of Christian history into a single ministerial constellation of bishop/priest/deacon.[3] The priesthood in time became the sole locus for official Christian ministry. Ministries grad-

---

3. The dynamics and motivations of this evolution are much debated. See for instance Chapters Three and Four of James Mohler's *The Origin and Evolution of the Priesthood* (New York: Alba House, 1970). For a more truculent interpretation of the hierarchizing and institutionalizing of Christian ministries see Ernst Kaesemann's "Ministry and Community in the New Testament," in *Essays on New Testament Themes* (Naperville, IL: Allenson, 1964), pp. 63–94. The intriguing disappearance of the ministry of prophecy is discussed in James Ash's "The Decline of Ecstatic Prophecy in the Early Church," *Theological Studies*, 37, no. 2 (June 1976): 227–252.

ually became one ministry, *priestly* ministry. Other Christians gave alms and performed charitable acts, but it was the priest who ministered. The use of the word *priest*, instead of servant or minister (both translations of the New Testament *diakonos*), indicated the reservation of official ministry to a restricted group of believers.

The Protestant reformation challenged this narrowed understanding of ministry, reminding the Church that all its members are called to a full participation in its mission. As part of its response to the reformation, the Roman Catholic Church established seminaries—both vastly improving the preparation of priests and further solidifying the distinction between priests as ministers and laity as those ministered to. This identification of ministry with priesthood, not evident in the New Testament or in the earliest communities, has been strongly challenged by Vatican II's emphasis on Baptism as calling each believer to a full involvement in the Church. The more restrictive view, however, does survive: the Vatican document on the question of the ordination of women, promulgated in 1976, speaks of "the priestly Order and ministry in its true sense" (art. 1).

Throughout the Catholic Church in America today a new, pluralist understanding of ministry is on the rise. Many lay Catholics working in educational and social service careers are beginning to think of themselves as involved in ministry; women religious describe themselves as ministers and many are moving into modes of parish and liturgical activity formerly reserved to priests. This quite different (for Catholics) understanding of ministry appears to result from two events in recent Catholic history. The first is the increasing shortage of priests, which has prompted the hierarchy to call other Catholics to be more involved in the ministry of the Church. The second cause is the laity's higher level of education and more assertive sense of involvement in the Church. In the hierarchical structure of the Catholic Church this need "from on high" (for more priests or ministers) and this need "from below" (the awakening of lay interest in formal ministry) have come together to turn upside down our traditional notions about ministry.

These movements in the Church invite us to take more seriously our Christian rhetoric of "the priesthood of the faithful."[4] We move

4. See Vatican II's Document on the Church (*Lumen Gentium*), Chapter Two, on the people of God where this "common priesthood of the faithful" is distinguished

in this direction as we help adults to learn how they are gifted for service—what specific thing each does well, what particular talent or insight each has to contribute to the development of the community. The pluriformity of these gifts pertains also to the degree of involvement. Not everyone is called to a formal, full-time role in the ministry, yet each of us is gifted for some kind of service in and beyond the community. Lay adults are recognizing that their own psychological and religious growth demands an active involvement in their community. It is inappropriate for an adult believer to remain a predominantly passive recipient of ministry: being a child of God does not entail remaining a child of the clergy.

As the different members of a believing community become more aware of their own gifts and their own adult need to serve, they also recognize more clearly the inappropriateness of requiring a single minister, the priest, to fulfill all the ministerial demands of the community. The pluralization of ministries need not destroy the rich heritage of the priesthood; it can result in greater clarity about the shape of this specific ministry and its location among the other ministries in the community.

The emergence of a variety of ministries is contributing in at least two ways to a more democratic and less hierarchical understanding of the community itself. First, when the priest as lone minister is replaced by a team of ministers, a model of collegial cooperation can be presented to the community. The truly collegial ministry team (where the team is not simply a group of "Father's helpers") can stand as a witness to the community of a variety of complementary gifts at work. Neither a mini-hierarchy of its own nor an expansion of the ministerial elite, such a team can illustrate a group of ministers whose different and limited gifts come together in a service that is truly communal. Second, this pluralism of ministries presents a model of members ministering to each

from the "ministerial or hierarchical priesthood." The unfortunate distinction of common and ministerial suggests that the priesthood of the faithful does not refer to their service in and beyond the community. In Vatican II's "Decree on the Apostolate of the Laity," great emphasis is laid on lay involvement in ministry according to their different gifts (Chapter One, art. 2). A note at the beginning of this document recalls an early suggestion, which the Council Fathers did not follow, to entitle the text "the participation of the laity in the mission of the Church." See Walter M. Abbott, ed., *The Documents of Vatican II* (New York: American Press, 1966), p. 489. Is the "priesthood of the faithful" only an honorific title which results from belonging to a "royal priesthood," or might it also be translated in terms of a Christian's participation in the ministry of Jesus Christ?

other. A lateral and mutual ministry among gifted and wounded believers replaces the vertical and hierarchical model of an *alter Christus* ministering to a needy but passive laity. With each believer called to serve in some way, professional ministry describes not a superior level of ministry or holiness, but the role of coordinating this variety of ministries within the community.

## Pluralism in Belief Itself

In the first section of this chapter we have pointed to a pluralism that is possible and even necessary in faith itself. Within the boundaries of orthodoxy, there is a variety of ways to say "Jesus is the Christ" and a variety of ways we celebrate liturgically the Lord's presence in the community. This pluriformity is grounded in the unspeakable richness of God-among-us.

Another more concrete and immediate expression of this pluriformity in our Christian belief today is the phrase "no one believes it all." This is really quite a simple statement. We are, each of us, gifted with only a partial understanding of God. Our vision is limited, our perspective flawed. This limitation in personal belief is set in a context of pluralism when we reflect on a community praying the Creed. The unity of our belief is expressed in the joining of voices in a public confession of faith. Yet upon examination we realize the variety of belief that supports this harmony of voices. One person in the congregation prays the Creed with an intense yet peaceful belief; another person utters the same words without really being present to their content; a third person prays in apparent unison but is in fact struggling against the doubt or despair growing in his heart. Three very different voices praying in harmony both represent and disguise three differing modes of belief. And this pluralism of belief is often reflected in the heart of the individual believer. Today this part of the Creed captures my attention, expressing powerfully my present relationship with the Lord. I pray this phrase with great energy and concentration. Later in this same communal prayer I pronounce a sentence that I want to believe, but from which I feel very distant. I do not so much deny this tenet of Christian faith as I feel unable to believe it with much conviction. But others in the group pray this with me, others who at this time believe more fully than I. These others will, in a sense, believe for me.

We begin to see here how a community differs from an individual. A community believes in a comprehensive fashion unavailable to the individual believer. This corporate belief completes my partial faith and makes up for my unbelief. In the fullest sense, it is the community that believes. It is this corporate belief (the faith of the whole Church) that is infallible, will not fail, is indefectible. Individual belief partakes of this strength as it participates in the discipline of community faith.

Relieved of this unrealistic expectation that each of us "believe it all," we can better acknowledge who we are as adult believers: each of us a combination of belief and unbelief, of strong convictions and some doubts. This state is not a peculiar failing of our own individual belief; it is, in fact, the profile of the adult Christian. With this more realistic and tolerant self-understanding we are, perhaps, less likely to submit to two temptations in adult belief: thinking that *my* understanding of Christian faith is the criterion against which others' orthodoxy is judged, or despairing in the weakness and inconstancy of my own faith. Here the ministry to such a pluralistic community becomes clearer. The goal is not simply to reduce diverse beliefs into single, lock-step unity, but to coordinate these plural beliefs and to strengthen individual faith by incorporation into the believing community.

If it is true that no one believes it all, it may also be true that no one believes all the time. This second realization has arisen as we have shifted our expectations about our own adult lives and human maturity. If we once believed that we should be, in adult life, stable and unchanging as proof of our maturity, we now recognize that maturity entails growth and even radical change. Such change is not always charted as a steady improvement, but is often initiated by disruption, loss, and personal failure. We mature and our faith deepens as we are tested, broken, and recast. As we become more familiar with our own and each other's adult faith, we more clearly recognize these patterns of change and become more tolerant of periods of unbelief.

"No one believes all the time." A concrete example may best illustrate this somewhat dramatic statement. Recently a good friend of ours, a professional minister in the Church, suffered a family tragedy. Struggling to deal with this loss, she came to feel she no longer believed in God, had lost her faith. As we listened to this not uncommon adult experience, we became aware of three possible responses to her grief. The first and most extreme would be to take this absence of faith literally and to advise her that, if she could no longer believe, then she was no longer a Christian. As a nonbeliever she no longer belongs in the community since it is, by definition, a community of faith.

A second response would be to deny the seriousness of her loss. Here a minister might say, "you didn't really lose your faith; you're just depressed; everything will be fine." This ministerial response intentionally ignores the gravity of the crisis, hoping to distract the person from the distress.

A third response attempts to take seriously both the loss of faith and the context of this loss—the person's life history as a believer and her location in a believing community. Her loss of faith is acknowledged; it is real. This tragedy has broken her trust in a loving God. But this "faithless" person is kept in community, in her traditional context of belief. Surrounded (but, it is hoped, not oppressively so) by believers, the person is given time to experience her unbelief and its causes, and to attend to its hoped-for revival. Here the believing community functions to sustain her through her unbelief: the community believes for her during this time. The strength and continuity of faith belong to the community. It sustains us and sees us through our own unbelief. And it does this not in some mystical fashion, but by showing us what belief is, surrounding us with all kinds of adults who continue to believe. When we come close to some of these believers, we see their faith with its scars and resilience. Such adult faith, as both wounded and mature, shows us the future of our own faith.

The community functions here in its proper role as sacrament: it witnesses to the possibility of belief, displays the faith of its members to us and by so doing invites us to greater and renewed faith. It effects what it signifies. The woman in the above example found her way in time to a new stage of faith. She survived the death of a more naive faith, a survival due, at least in part, to a community of brother and sister believers who sustained her through her unbelief.

To translate this assertion "no one believes all the time" in a less dramatic fashion, we may simply note the plural stages of faith in an individual life. An adolescent way of believing gives way to a more adult faith; this mode of believing is further matured by the insights, losses, and graces of later decades. The transitions between these stages are, for many, accompanied by a disruption of the person's former faith. One accustomed way of relating to God is broken to allow for another, more mature relationship. The dangers that attend such a movement of growth through loss are tamed by the community that surrounds us with faith and care, predicting our survival. Such a community both believes in us and believes for us.

These two expectations—that we should, each of us, believe it all and believe all the time—are grounded in an excessive individualism. We Americans like to be independent and self-sufficient. Should we not be able to take care of ourselves in our faith life, too? Such heroic and individualistic expectations contribute to a vision of a community as a composition of self-sufficient adults: similarly mature individuals are repeated throughout the group. This ideal of uniform self-sufficiency neglects the complementarity which, in fact, constitutes a community. It is this supportive and challenging complementarity which rescues us from our individualism and incorporates us into communal belief.

## Conclusion

We have argued in this chapter for a more explicit celebration of the pluralism in the believing community. If some of the diversity in our common life arises from ignorance and sinful antagonism, pluriformity in many instances points to the richness of God's presence among us.

The experience of pluralism within the faith community today is bounded by two other experiences of pluralism: the different religious faiths in the world and the pluriformity within the individual believer. The pluralism of faiths in the world, though always a fact, has only in recent times attracted the serious attention of Christians. The "one, true faith" has at last become aware that ignorance and heresy are not sufficient categories to understand other religious traditions, such as Buddhism and Islam. Nor can we understand their gracefulness as merely Christianity in disguise, as the activity of "anonymous Christians." Exposure to others who are not Christians, yet who live deeply religious and faith-filled lives, is inviting Christian theology to a more pluralistic understanding of God's action in the world. The religious pluralism of the world community both increases our anxiety over those who are religiously other and gives added urgency to the need to more carefully and maturely bring together the plural families of God.

Another pluralism coming to awareness today is that within the individual adult believer. The discontinuity and incompleteness of our own personal faith, discussed in the section above, is related to a profound shift in our interpretation of our adult lives. Increased life expectancy in the past century has doubled the length of adult life. This lengthening has made us more aware of different stages in adult life, with these stages resulting in a plural sense of self as we mature as adults and as Christians. Beyond this longitudinal pluralism of self, we are more comfortable today in admitting the different forces that are at play, or at war, within us right now. Luther's phrase "at once saved and a sinner" has an intriguing contemporary ring to it. Adult maturity invites me to find a greater comfort with my own plural and unfinished self. Christian asceticism entails not only a lifelong effort to overcome and root out sinful parts of myself, but a similarly long effort to befriend the confusing, limited, unhealed parts of who I am. Religious maturity emerges in our gradual befriending of this ambiguity and pluralism within our own interior lives.

Ambiguities and unclarities abound in Christian life today: women wish for ordination to the priesthood; Christians who are gay seek a more thorough inclusion in the community and in ministry; church leaders preach poverty while some seem to live in near luxury. Will these ambiguities cripple our faith? Must they be denied or resolved in quick, defensive fashion? Or can we tolerate such ambiguity and continue to listen to the plural information about these questions as it arises in the faith community and in society?

Pluralism—within Christian belief, among religious traditions, and even within ourselves—will not soon go away. If we can see beyond the potential, and often real, scandal of this diversity, while refusing to use pluralism as a dodge to avoid genuine confrontation, we may be able to find ways to celebrate pluralism in our communities as a sign of the richness and the endlessly diverse presence of God among us.

## FOR FURTHER REFLECTION

In a prayerful mood, return in your imagination to sacred scripture. Recall the images and phrases and stories of the Old and New Testaments that speak to you of community. Take time with this first recollective phase, bringing to mind some of the scripture's richness concerning community. Then select one of these images and spend time in reflection.

1. What does this image (or phrase or story) offer to heal your own experience of community?

2. What does this image from scripture offer to challenge or overturn your current expectations of community?

3. What does this image offer to enliven your hopes for community?

Close this reflection with a moment of prayer, holding yourself open before the Word of God that speaks to you now.

## ADDITIONAL RESOURCES

The diversity of the early Christian communities is being examined closely by biblical scholars today. In *The Community of the Beloved Disciple*, (New York: Paulist Press, 1979) Raymond Brown explores the "life, loves, and hates" of the Christians among whom the fourth gospel was composed. Robert Banks discusses the historical context of the early house churches to which Paul ministered in *Paul's Idea of Community* (Grand Rapids, MI: Wm. B. Eerdmans Publishing Co., 1980). Eugene LaVerdiere and William Thompson focus on the gospel accounts of Matthew and Luke in their analysis, "New Testament Communities," in *Why the Church?* (New York: Paulist Press, 1978), edited by William G. Thompson and Walter J. Burghardt.

The rich pluralism in contemporary theological research can be seen in two important recent contributions in Christology: Edward Schillebeeckx's *Jesus; An Experiment in Christology* (New York: Crossroad Publishing Co., 1979) and Jon Sobrino's *Christology at the Crossroads* (New York: Orbis Books, 1978). Edward Braxton suggests a pastoral framework for dealing with the often confusing diversity of contemporary church life in *The Wisdom Community* (New York: Paulist Press, 1980). In our book *Method in Ministry: Theological Reflection and Christian Ministry* (New York: The Seabury Press, 1980), we outline a process of community reflection that recognizes pluralism as a communal resource.

# ✤ PART II

## CLARIFYING THE MEANING OF COMMUNITY

# 2 ❖
# Community Is a Way
# to Be Together

The challenge of community is alive in the Church today. We see it in many places. Christians unhappy with the impersonality and bureaucracy of official church life seek out informal groupings of like-minded believers with whom they can share their religious life and hopes. Parishes experiment with neighborhood subgroupings in an attempt to nourish a sense of belonging and mutual commitment among members. Women and men in ministry establish collaborative work teams and peer support groups. Religious congregations stress anew the value of their life in common as a sign of the gospel promise of community—and struggle to make this sign a practical reality in their local houses and institutions. Dioceses attempt to develop structures which encourage the exercise of shared authority and collegial responsibility among bishops, priests, and people. And theologians work to develop an ecclesiology that takes seriously the implications, both for the Church's life and for its self-understanding, of the Vatican II statements concerning the Church as the people of God.

Attempts to enliven the experience of community within the Church have not been easy. Nor, in the experience of many people, have they been very successful. Several reasons are offered to explain the difficulty of the move toward greater community in church life and religious organizations: numbers, apathy, mobility, time, polarization, inertia, even "bad will." The explanation, perhaps, runs deeper.

Philip Slater, a perceptive critic of the American scene, has underscored a contemporary ambivalence regarding community. On the one hand, many of us feel keenly the desire for community, for the chance to share with others our own life and work, as a part of an identifiable group of people who are bound together by trust and cooperation. Yet, equally strong among us is the influence of the American cultural commitment to individualism and the autonomous pursuit of one's own destiny.

American Christians share in this contradictory experience and in the ambivalence that results. We want the support that comes from belonging to a group of people who share our religious values, but we resent group restraints. We want to participate in groups that enable us to feel "at home" in a complex and often confusing public world, but we are wary of group demands and suspicious of elitism and exclusivity. It is in the context of this ambivalence, then, that the religious call to community has been heard.

**Community—An Unclear Ideal**

The term "community" is itself vague and diffuse. To some people the word suggests an experience of interdependence. It seems to call for a return to the kind of social relationships that are thought—perhaps only nostalgically—to have characterized small-town America or the ethnically defined urban neighborhood. This "community as neighborhood" model is supported by the definition of parish, the local unit of church life, in terms of geographic and territorial boundaries.

Other people focus on different connotations of the word. Their expectations of Christian community include the development of close interpersonal ties in an atmosphere of emotional honesty and mutual support. Here it is "community as support group" which is stressed.

These two understandings of community are not necessarily opposed, but neither are they always in harmony. The religious language about community contributes to the complexity. When the Church calls its people to community—in its official documents, in its liturgical texts and homilies—it often does so in images of the family. Jesus has taught us to call God "Father"; we belong to "Holy Mother Church." Christ's intimate care for this Church has been often imaged as the love of a husband for his wife. These family relationships fill our imaginations as we struggle to live together in Christian community. As powerful as these images are—touching our deepest aspirations for love, communion and care—they may also be confusing when we attempt to translate our religious ideals into our practical life together in a parish or religious congregation.

For many of us, the family is not the most useful image of an adult community. When we think of a family or, more significantly, when the images and emotions of our own past experiences of family life are evoked, the most influential memories are likely to be of ourselves as young children growing up in the powerful presence (or absence) of our own mothers and fathers. Over the years of active child rearing in the home, children and parents are bound together in many significant and satisfying ways, but they are not "equals." These early parent-child relations may be marked by considerable care and much love on both sides, but they are not likely to represent patterns that will be appropriate in an adult community of faith.

The movement through adolescence and into more independent adulthood involves, for many of us, some renegotiation of our earlier relationships with our parents in the direction of a greater sense of adult mutuality. We attempt to reestablish our connectedness with them, but now as adult with adult. These renegotiated family relationships may hold clues to the processes of belonging and commitment suitable for the adult community in the Church. But it is seldom this sense of mutuality among adults that the image of family evokes.

Even more significantly, in the experience and imagination of most Americans, the family is not a model of social involvement with others. It is rather the most obvious arena of "private life." Family is a place of security and privacy. Here I can find relief from the multiple demands of my public responsibilities. It is in the family that my subjectivity is nourished; I can let down my defenses and just be myself.

But community is about more than private life. Community, as we shall see more clearly in the chapters ahead, is not simply a synonym for intimate self-disclosure and emotional support. Self-disclosure and support are, in most instances, elements of groups that experience themselves as communities—but more is involved. Community is a goal of social life; it points to the possibility of a shared vision that can move us to action in a public sphere, undertaken in a context of mutual concern.

How, then, to move from the religious images of community as family toward workable models of life together in our parishes, congregations, institutions, and ministry teams? It is this question that leads us into a discussion of community as a style of group life.

## Community as a Style of Group Life

"The goal of the ministry team this year is to have St. Mark's become a community."

"The entire community shall be assessed for the construction of the new road."

"My main concern is that there is no community for me in this work."

"Three of us in the community are school teachers; the other two sisters are in parish work."

"I joined this team for a community; instead, we have become an organization."

"Lord, we gather as a community at your table."

Community—the term has many meanings and is often used without a precise definition in mind. We can indicate two common uses of the word in ordinary conversation. Sometimes *community* is used to mark a special quality we experience in relationships among people. Where there is a sense of belonging, an awareness of support, a recognition that we have much in common—here there is community. This use of *community* to point to these feelings of solidarity might be considered a psychological use of the word. But there is another, somewhat different, sense to *community*. Some groups of people—a parish, a neighborhood, a religious congregation—are called communities. Here the word signifies a style or structure of group life. We might call this the sociological use of the term. We say *community* here not so much to point to the feelings of fellowship and solidarity, but to designate the group's formal structure or the ways these people are brought together.

These two orientations to community are, of course, closely related: living in a community structure, we hope to come to an experience of closeness and commitment. Yet the *structure* and the *experience* of community can be separated: we may experience strong, intimate bonds with persons no longer living near us; we may also participate in a community structure that is devoid of mutual acceptance and fellowship.

It is the sociological understanding of community as a form or style of group life that we shall explore in the next five chapters. Our goal is to examine the patterns—the recurring activities, the emerging values, the developing relationships—that characterize those groups that do function as communities for their participants.

**Community as an Intermediate Group Style**

The social life of most adults is complex. Many of us are aware of this complexity. We are a part of several worlds; we participate in a number of different kinds of groups. Helen Rigali, for example, is a member of three groups that are very important to her. For Helen, her family is the most immediate and the most important group in her life. She and her husband have been married for eighteen years; they are raising two teenage daughters and a son still in grade school. Recently Helen has gone from part-time to full-time status as a sales agent with a large real estate company. Her contract with the firm is quite clear: specific goals and obligations define her role in this organization. She enjoys her work—even though it is often tiring—and she especially appreciates the opportunity it provides for her to interact regularly with the other sales persons. Helen is also a long-time member of St. Matthew's parish. She and her husband share a renewed sense of commitment to this group of Christians and an enthusiasm for a new sense of belonging and action that has developed in the parish over the last several years. Helen is concerned about the time demands that will come with her new full-time work status. If her evenings and weekends are no longer free, will her sense of involvement at St. Matthew's be lost? For that matter, she is beginning to sense some discomfort among the kids over her being away so much when they are home. Each of these groups is important for Helen, although in different ways. But they all make demands—on her energies, her commitment, and especially her time.

One of the important tools that sociologists use to understand this complexity of social life is the image of a continuum. This continuum extends from the primary group at one pole—a small, cohesive grouping with strong ties among members and a wide range of shared interests—to, at the other pole, the association—a more formal organization with explicit structures of rights and obligations. Examples of primary groups are a family, a household, or a close-knit group of friends. Formal associations would include large organizations, such as General Motors or IBM, and other task-oriented groups, such as a United Way fund-raising committee or, as in Helen's example, a real estate agency.

*Community* is a term that refers to ways for people to be together, patterns of group interaction, that fall in the large middle area on the continuum. The word *community* designates intermediate social forms.

**Figure 2.1**

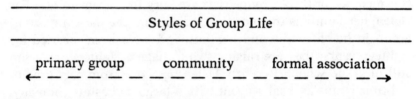

Styles of Group Life

primary group      community      formal association

Since it lies midway along the continuum, we can expect that the group style of community will include some of the elements that are found at either pole. A community is similar to a primary group in some ways, but also different. And, on the other hand, a community has characteristics that make it both like and different from a formal association. Often the religious discussion of community stresses the ways in which community differs from a formal organization. Perhaps in reaction against what we sense was an over-organization of much of church life in the past, we want to come together more spontaneously now, with fewer rules and roles to tell us how we are to deal with each other. We want to gather in smaller groupings with like-minded persons with whom we feel ourselves emotionally compatible, especially on the religious values that are most important to us personally—whether these be worship or justice or spirituality or reconciliation. These goals stress some of the "primary group" elements that may be present in the community of faith. But to appreciate the distinctiveness of community it is necessary, as well, to note the ways in which communities differ from primary relationships.

*A Community Is Not Simply a Primary Group*

As a style of group life, community is similar to a primary group in several ways. Persons who are together in community are likely to develop emotional ties. The level of personal communication in a community will foster a sense of belonging. Social cohesion is important for a community, as it is for a primary group.

But a community will differ in important ways from the model of a family or other primary group: in size, in intensity, in diversity.

• In size. Primary groups must be small enough to allow face-to-face interaction among all members on a regular basis. Membership in a community need not involve each person in face-to-face interaction with all other members.

• In intensity. A primary group, due in part to its size, can sustain a high level of emotional exchange and personal sharing among all members. In most cases, this kind of sharing is not a realistic model for personal sharing among members of a community.

• In diversity. The size and interpersonal demands of primary groups both require and produce high levels of compatibility among group members. Often one of the reasons that a group begins to form—or that people begin to want regular and continuing relationships with each other—is because they recognize similarities: "These people are like me." On the other hand, people who do spend a good deal of time together, who share the same milieu of interests and values, tend to *become* more alike over time. The opportunity for—the pressure for—homogeneity among group members is likely to be greater the more close-knit the group. And consequently, coping with diversity is likely to be a bigger problem. Many groups, on the other hand, seek diversity among their members—diversity of experience, interests, orientation, skills, age, or values. A modern hospital or university, for example, would be brought to a standstill if similarity of skills or interests were the prime consideration in who could work there. In many instances communities require diversity and pluralism to ensure their growth, survival, and effectiveness.

*Communities Are Not Simply Associations*

As a style of social life, a community is also similar to an association. It is likely that the focus of a community (more so than is the case in a family or other primary group) will include goals and interests that go beyond the group itself. Thus the members of a ministry team are together not just for themselves, but for a work in which they share. Interaction within a community will usually require more explicit understanding of the rights and responsibilities of membership than is the case in a primary group. A potluck supper among a group of friends may succeed with only an informal sense of "who will bring what." A successful effort in team ministry is more likely to require a clear awareness of the responsibilities of each member.

But communities also differ in important ways from associations. An individual is involved in a formal organization through a specific role (for example, as teacher, brick-layer, ticket agent). This role is that part of the person's total self which performs the task or service for which the organization was established. Involvement in a community is not limited to just one specialized role. More of the individual can be known within the group, more of the person's personality and values can be shared.

**The Parish as Community**

These considerations clarify the sense in which a parish or a congregation may be said to function in the social style of community. Members of a parish share concern for the religious dimensions of their lives—their experiences of God, of prayer and transcendence, of need and justice, of sin and salvation. This religious concern moves parishioners to come together in various ways—to worship, to share their hopes and doubts of God's movement in their lives, to plan for the religious education of their children, to act together in the cause of justice and peace. As a community, the parish is like an organization since it involves members in goals and activities that reach beyond their intimate circle of family and close friends. The parish has a mission. Its task is to nourish its own religious life so that it may act beyond itself both in word and in deed, witnessing to the saving presence of God in the world. Some of its activities will be structured and routinized in committees, councils, and agencies. These organizational steps are not undertaken for their own sake, but in order that the religious purposes of the parish may be served more efficiently and effectively. Parish organization, like organization in business and elsewhere, may sometimes seem to complicate rather than to serve the larger goals of the group. But a parish community without any organizational elements would lack an important foundation for its communication and growth.

But the parish community also differs from an organization. An individual's involvement in the parish need not be limited to one specialized organizational role. "More" of the person can come into play. A parish is thus similar to a primary group since it allows and even expects personal involvement and commitment among its members. But its larger size, its more formal structures of communication and responsibility, its ongoing concern for a mission that includes but goes beyond the maintenance and social cohesion of the group itself—these essential elements of parish life make many characteristics of primary relationships inappropriate as goals of a parish community. A parish community can be made up of a number of closely knit smaller (primary) groupings—families, neighborhood clusters, prayer groups. But the level of friendship within these small groups will be different than the communication that can go on among members of the parish as a whole.

**The Religious Congregation as Community**

This understanding of community as an intermediate form of group life may also be applied to congregations of vowed religious. There are many ways in which the religious congregation as a whole resembles a formal association. It is a legal entity, with explicit structures of authority and responsibility and stated norms governing the rights and duties (financial and otherwise) of membership. But religious congregations are not simply formal associations. They are voluntarily formed groups of adults who come together for mutual support in a shared religious mission. To the congregation as a whole, the internal focus (mutual encouragement and challenge) and the external focus (a mission of witness and action in the world) are both of significance. But local houses of religious congregations often differ among themselves in the balance between these two goals. Some function toward the "primary group" pole of the continuum, as small, close-knit groups of religious whose principal function is to support and challenge one another in personal and spiritual growth. Each person is likely to be involved in ministry, but there is not a group ministry in which all share. In other religious houses there is an attempt to combine both functions. Members share a common ministry (in a parish or school or project) as well as a commitment to mutual challenge and support. This living arrangement makes additional demands on all the members, but—when it succeeds—can also provide the advantages of increased collaboration and a strong communal witness. When the attempt to combine common ministry and common residence fails, however, it can lead to frustration both at home and work.

### The Ministry Team as Community

A team of colleagues in ministry may function as a community. Such a group will be small, manifest a high level of social cohesion, and encourage honest emotional exchange among members—all characteristics that move it toward primary group functioning. It will distinguish itself from a primary group, however, in the importance that members of the team give to the accomplishment of a task in ministry.

Not all teams in ministry are, or stay, communities. There is a tension involved. If the pull of the primary relationships is strong, if members look more and more to the group for personal support and emotional sustenance, the group may become chiefly a support group for the members and not, as a group, involved in a corporate task beyond the group itself. This is not, necessarily, a bad thing. It may be the most appropriate development for a particular group at a particular time. But it does entail a movement away from the social style of community toward the social style of primary group. On the other hand, a team may find the interpersonal issues too distracting, or too time-consuming, or too threatening. Members may opt, consciously or unconsciously, for more formal, limited, work-oriented relationships with each other. The decision to focus the team's interaction more exclusively on the task need not mean that their relationships must deteriorate to the level of anonymity or animosity. But such a decision will move the group closer to the social style of an association or organization. Such a group of coworkers may describe their collaboration as that of a staff rather than a team. In some situations this is the most appropriate model for working together in ministry.

There are many varieties of collaborative working relationships that exist in ministry today. Not all of these do include, or need to include, the expectation that those who are involved in ministry together in some way will function as a community. But more and more there is an interest among those working together in ministry to be more than simply a well-organized staff. (Often enough, to be sure, those in ministry together experience themselves to be a good deal *less* than a well-organized staff!)

**Community Takes Many Forms**

The examples we have considered here demonstrate that there is not just one shape to community—there are many. There is not just one way to bring people together, one pattern for organizing their interaction with each other, one best structure to guide their communication, one model that can guarantee success. Some effective communities will look a good deal like primary groups, with serious attention given to the group itself and high expectations of sharing and mutual support. Other effective communities will function more as organizations, with greater focus on a goal outside the group and more limited expectations of emotional exchange. A style of community interaction that suits a prayer group of six or eight people will, most likely, be inappropriate as a model of what should go on among staff members in a social service agency who wish to make their interaction more communal.

Community, then, is not a univocal term. Within the broad category of groups that function as communities there will be noticeable differences from group to group. Some of these differences are related to a group's history. For example, groups which initially are not communities may take steps to become more communal in their style. A primary group of close friends can decide to work together for a task (for example, developing a cooperative day-care center for their children) and gradually specify more explicitly the range of responsibilities among them. They remain committed to their values of friendship and mutual support and now attempt to supplement these with a shared commitment to action. At the other pole of group styles, a formally constituted task group (such as a school faculty) may decide to take more seriously the larger life and development of the members, and move toward a wider range of personal support and interaction among themselves.

The social styles that emerge in these two instances may differ considerably, but each may appropriately be considered a community, an intermediate social form. Thus *community* does not point to one particular structure of group life. Rather, the term refers to a range of social forms, a variety of patterns of interaction and communication within groups. One group will incorporate several elements and expectations of primary relations. Another will show more concern for formal patterns of organization. But each may be understood as an intermediate style of group life, as a community.

Large groupings of religious people—a suburban parish, for example, or a religious congregation with several hundred members—will include a wide range of group styles. There will be primary groups, intermediate communities, and more task-oriented organizations—each serving a different need within the religious life of the group, each an appropriate style of interaction for religious people. There is sometimes the tendency, perhaps even the temptation, among religious people to think of community exclusively in its primary group connotation. But surely the Christian witness of working together unceasingly—even if not always easily—to hasten the coming of the Kingdom stands equal to the Christian witness of the love we bear one another as a sign to the world of God's presence among us.

## FOR FURTHER REFLECTION

What are the images and experiences that influence your own awareness of community? Two exercises may help to achieve a clearer sense of these personal meanings.

1. "For me, community is . . ."
   In a quiet atmosphere, reflect on this phrase and take note of the different words and images that come to mind. It will be useful to write down these responses. Stay with the exercise until you have completed the phrase several times.

   Then look back over your responses. What image or understanding of community emerges from your list? Is there a dominant mood or attitude? What do you learn here about your own expectations of community?

**2.** Next, consider the groups to which you belong, the people with whom you participate on a regular basis. It may help to write down the names of the persons who are with you in each of these group settings.

After you have taken some time to list these groups, ask yourself the question: Is any of these groups a community for you? Which group(s)? Why? Spend some time examining the things that indicate community to you; be as concrete as you can. What does it mean for this group to be a community? What actions or behaviors do you point to? What feelings or convictions are part of your experience of community in this group?

## ADDITIONAL RESOURCES

Bishop Albert Ottenweller, Paula Ripple, John Shea, Gerard Egan, Philip Murnion, and Daniel Coughlin, all contributors to the volume *The Parish in Community and Ministry*, edited by Evelyn Eaton Whitehead (New York; Paulist Press, 1978), take up a number of issues central to parish community and examine these from both theological and social science perspectives. Charles Keating initiates a dialogue between Christian spirituality and the behavioral sciences in *Community: Learning to Live in Diocesan, Religious and Parish Communities* (St. Meinrad, IN: Abbey Press, 1977). Karl Rahner discusses the movement of base community churches in *Concern for the Church*, Theological Investigations XX (New York: Crossroads Publishing Co., 1981). In their chapter "Community-Formation and the Church" in *Faith and Society* (Louvain: University of Louvain, 1978), edited by M. Caudron, European social scientists K. Dobbelaere and J. Billiet provide a comprehensive analysis of the variety of religiously motivated efforts toward community in Belgium. There is much in each of these considerations that is relevant to the Church in the United States.

In *The Pursuit of Loneliness* (Boston: Beacon Press, 1970), Philip Slater offers a provocative discussion of the tensions generated by contradictions in contemporary American experience. The strain arises in our culture's commitment to three mutually antagonistic sets of ideals: competition/community; engagement/isolation; and independence/interdependence. Although many of his examples are drawn from the 1960s, his discussion continues to throw light on the complexity of efforts to develop religious community. Over the decade which followed, Richard Sennett has taken up the discussion of the contemporary images of autonomy and community that influence American social life in *The Fall of Public Man* (New York: Vintage Books, 1978) and *Authority* (New York: Vintage Books, 1981).

# 3 ❖
# Basic Questions of Group Life

There is a series of questions that may be asked of any group that intends to function as a community for its members. These questions serve as a base for clarifying experiences and expectations regarding Christian life together. They are not intended to elicit the "correct" answer, to point to the "one right way" to bring about community. On the contrary, they should lead to the awareness that there are various ways for communities to function. The questions can guide an examination of the patterns that actually exist within groups that hope to be communities, focusing attention on those dimensions that are critical to any group's life. In this way the analytic framework provided by the sociology of community can contribute to the religious mission of community formation.

These questions may be asked about the functioning of any group:

1. What is the major focus of this group?
2. How fully is the individual member expected to be involved with this group?
3. How appropriate is it for the members of this group to share with one another on an emotional level?
4. How is behavior regulated in this group?
5. How obligated are members to each other and to the group as a whole?
6. How are evaluations made about persons who are members of the group?

Our first goal in asking these questions is clarification: we want to understand how a particular group does, in fact, function. Later it may be desirable to ask how *satisfied* we are with the way this group is operating—whether, for example, the group meets the expectations of its members or the obligations of its charter. But such evaluation, necessary as it is, should remain a subsequent goal. The first task is to describe the group as accurately as possible, to become aware of how it functions in several critical areas. Here we will consider each of the questions, giving some examples of how different groups respond. As we go through the questions it may be useful for the reader to look at each in terms of a particular group that he or she knows well.

### What Is the Major Focus of The Group?

Sometimes the main reason a group comes together is for the group itself. The activities of the group are directed chiefly toward the needs and interests of its members. Examples here could include a family household, a circle of friends, a group of drinking buddies, even a more formally constituted support group.

But there are other situations in which the focus of a group's activities or the reason that the group has initially come together lies outside the group—a task to be done, a product to be made, a set of purposes to be achieved. So a critical focus of a factory production team, a university curriculum committee, or a United Way fund-raising group will be the accomplishment of a task—one that goes beyond the group itself.

The question of focus concerns the priority that a group establishes between its internal life and its external goals. It is rare that any group goes for very long with only internal interests or external goals. Some combination of internal and external focus is much more likely. Within the family, for example, parents are concerned about providing an atmosphere of discipline and encouragement that will help their children do well in school. A factory foreman knows that when the workers on his shift get along well with one another and with him, they are both more satisfied and more productive, so he forms a company softball team. Finding the balance of internal and external focus is an important part of any group's life. And over the course of that life, the focus of a group can shift. Thus a group of friends (primarily an internal focus) may decide to buy stock together or to collaborate in the renovation of their neighborhood (taking on some external goals). Members of a local

Parent-Teacher Association may find, through their collaboration in raising money for their school (a task with external goals), that they enjoy each other's company (more internal focus) and so decide to have their families vacation together.

The response to a question concerning the degree of internal or external focus in any particular group will fall along a continuum, indicating the relative importance to the group of its internal life and its external task.

### How Fully Are Members Involved?

A second dimension of group life concerns the incorporation of the individual within the group. The question here is "how much" of the individual member is available to the group. What is at issue is not so much commitment as comprehensiveness: I may feel *deeply committed* to my job, yet only a *limited range* of my total personality may come into play in the work setting. The "how much" we are examining here, then, is measured more in breadth than in depth.

Before we explore this "how much" question in groups, let us note some differences in one-to-one relationships. In some relationships (a friendship, for example) I may share a good deal of myself—my ideas and emotions, my memories of the past and my hopes for the future. In other relationships less of my total personality comes into play. With an acquaintance in the neighborhood I may exchange greetings and perhaps other small courtesies— keeping an eye on each other's house or taking in the mail when one or the other is out of town. But neither of us wants or expects the relationship to develop beyond this.

There are similar differences in our participation in groups. Among a group of friends there is the general sense that we bring much of ourselves to the interaction. There may, of course, be areas of privacy that are maintained. I may not want to bring up a troubled relationship within my family; you may have a keen sense of confidentiality about some things that go on in your work. But we expect the give-and-take among us when we gather as a group of friends to cover a range of common interests and to include sharing on several levels. "More" of me is available in this group than, for example, in a local meeting of the political party to which I belong. In a political caucus it is a more limited range of my person that is likely to become involved. This group engages my interests within a narrower scope. The goals I share with others here may be very important to me—honesty in government, improved local services in our neighborhood, a court system that safeguards basic human rights—but I do not expect to share much of my broader life interests within this group.

In some groups, then, members are more completely integrated, with a wide range of their personalities, talents, values and emotions available in group interaction (such as is the case in a family, sorority, or commune). In other groups, members are involved partially and instrumentally, through explicit roles (as "first-grade teacher" or "committee member" or "employee"). It is important to note again that this question does not deal precisely with the issue of personal commitment or the extent of my appreciation for this group. It is not a motivational but a structural point that is at issue. I may be a very committed member of a local neighborhood improvement group; I may attend meetings regularly, contribute financially, volunteer a good deal of time to projects that further the group's goals. But only a portion of my larger personality is engaged here. The weekend party that brings together a group of old friends may lack the focus of the block club meeting, but it has a range of broader personal involvement, at least potentially. Such a group depends on this wide involvement of its members, an involvement not limited to the performance—even the excellent performance—of a specific activity. It is not enough that I show up on time for the party with my share of the food. My friends will expect me to be present to them, to contribute to the festive mood, to be "available" in ways that are difficult to specify ahead of time.

There are some groups in which it is unnecessary for members to share much of each other's lives. As a stamp collector, I may be a regular and enthusiastic member of the local philatelists' club. But there are many parts of my life that are irrelevant to my role as stamp collector and thus are "outside" the group's experience of me. It is not that I am "holding back"; it is not that the other group members are "inhibiting me." Rather it is that my participation in this group is partial, and correctly so.

There are other group settings in which it is even inappropriate for members to expect a wider range of personal exchange. A citizens' review board, a jury, a fund-raising group, a neighborhood clean-up committee might be examples. In each of these groups, only a part of me is involved in pursuit of the goal I share with the other group members.

The same is true in many church-related groupings. To be an effective member of the parish school board or the social action committee, it is not necessary that I become a close friend of all the other members or that I see this group as the people with whom I chose to spend my free time. Ideally, we will not view each other as strangers, but our communication and collaboration may well have a particular and somewhat limited goal. This limited goal does not mean that our relationships in parish groups of this kind cannot be warm and personally significant. We may, in fact, choose to pray together regularly or to meet socially from time to time. Rather it recalls for us the rich variety of relationship styles that are a part of adult life. In Chapter 9 we shall discuss in greater detail the ways in which a variety of styles of communication and care can contribute to community.

Finally, the question of "how fully involved" is not meant to suggest a norm of total involvement in all groups. It is, instead, an attempt to understand and describe group diversity in relation to the extent to which members' total personalities are integrated into the life of the group.

**Is Emotional Sharing Appropriate among Us?**

This third question examines the place of emotions in the life of the group. There are groups in which the expression of feelings is an important and expected aspect of communication—among friends, between loved ones, within certain counseling relationships. In such groups it is not merely acceptable to share at an affective or emotional level; the relationship actually requires this exchange. In a relationship characterized by personal intimacy and emotional depth there can be a sense of disappointment, even hurt, when some special joy or sorrow is witheld. There is a legitimate expectation that these emotional aspects of life will be shared, even though such trust continues to be experienced as a gift.

Many of us have had an experience like this. I spend a pleasant evening with an old friend whom I have not seen in a while. Over a leisurely dinner we get caught up on the details of each other's life, discuss some of the things we are each involved with in our jobs, and share some laughs. The evening together has been fun. Several days later I learn from someone else that my friend is in the midst of a difficult time in her ministry. I feel concern for her and I also realize that I feel somehow "left out." It is not that she "owes it to me" to share that part of her life, but there is a sense of disappointment. I want to support her in this difficult time; perhaps there is something I can do to help. Most of all, I wish she could have trusted me enough to share with me her distress.

In other relationships there is not such an expectation of emotional sharing. There are groups in which such an exchange would be considered out of place. We can all recall the uneasiness we experience in a group when someone moves to a level of emotional communication or self-disclosure that is sensed to be inappropriate—when at a board meeting of a civic group, for example, a member starts to discuss what she likes and dislikes about her psychiatrist, or when a participant in a meeting of the liturgy committee moves into sharing his dismay over his marital problem.

In some groups very little emotional exchange is expected or permitted. In other groups only positive or only negative emotions are encouraged. The unspoken code of business colleagues, for example, may permit the exchange of only their success stories; among a group of teens it may be only their negative experiences of teachers and parents that can be shared.

In still other groups there may be other restrictions or guidelines on the exchange of personal feeling. These may be limited to particular times (holidays, funerals) or to particular places (taverns, locker rooms). Although groups will differ in regard to their expectations of emotional exchange, this affective dimension remains one of the key elements of group life.

### How Is Group Behavior Regulated?

A fourth critical dimension of group life concerns the manner in which behavior is influenced in the group. The question here is not *whether* behavior is influenced: my behavior is always influenced by the persons with whom I interact. The question is rather that of *manner*—*how* is this regulation accomplished? How do members know what kinds of behavior are expected of them? In some groups the means of regulation are implicit rather than formally stated. No list of "do's" and "don'ts" is drawn up and passed around, but people in the group are nevertheless aware of what is expected of them. In many groups, then, social control is most often achieved through group pressure or the influence of custom and tradition. The other members of the group communicate to me, sometimes in ways about which none of us is especially aware, that certain of my actions or attitudes are acceptable, even desirable, while others are not. A smile or a frown, commendation or ridicule, and—especially—inclusion or isolation works powerfully to shape the behavior of persons in the group. Through these and other influences there develops a shared, though largely implicit, understanding of "how we do things around here."

In other groups the mechanisms of social influence are more explicit. Statements of procedure are drawn up, bylaws are formulated, laws are promulgated—with the intention of making clear the range of behavior acceptable within the group.

Most groups regulate the behavior of members both implicitly and explicitly. For example, we have a set of guidelines we give to new teachers detailing their rights and obligations as members of this faculty, and we also urge them to take their lunch in the faculty lounge so that they can meet the other teachers in an informal setting and get a better sense of the spirit and morale at Central Catholic High.

To understand any particular group, it helps to understand the ways in which the behavior of its members is influenced and the degree to which these influences are implicit or explicit. Such an analysis does not start from the premise that either form of influence is better or more effective. A statement clearly defining the boundaries of acceptable activity will be influential and useful in many situations. Both parents and their adolescent children, for instance, may find that getting the rules of the house down on paper can reduce any tension between them on questions of discipline. Or a subcommittee of the Priests' Senate may be commissioned to clarify for the whole diocese some of the issues of clerical dress, leisure-time activities, vacation planning, and continuing education that have been found to be trouble spots between newly ordained priests and their first pastors.

But this is not to deny the power of a group's unspoken norms or unwritten customs to keep behavior within certain bounds. We can each of us testify to the power of a group's implicit regulation, coming up with instances when we changed our behavior or modified an opinion in response to what we sensed to be strong— but often unstated—pressure to do so. Recalling ourselves so pressured, we may consider the implicit regulation of group norms and custom to be generally harmful. But the processes of group life are more complex than this. While examples of the negative effects of social pressure are easy to cite, these tell only part of the tale. As most psychologists and many effective leaders know, group influence is an important, even necessary factor in most experiences of personal change and growth. (We will spend more time in consideration of the relations between group life and change in Chapter 6.) And while a group's living customs may rigidify into inflexible and no longer useful conventions that govern "how we do it around here," in many instances this vital sense of what is customary among us is much more open to development and flexibility than are explicitly formulated laws and regulations.

**How Obligated Are We to One Another?**

A further element of importance concerns the scope of the obligation that group membership entails. In some groups the obligation that exists among members is broad and diffuse. There is a wide range of rights and duties that members have in relation to each other, and some of these are not easy to list in advance. The commitments of the traditional wedding ceremony express this kind of diffuse mutual obligation—"in sickness and in health, for richer and for poorer, until death do us part." Our responsibilities to one another are not defined by or limited to any one set of particular actions. Rather, we are each obligated to do "whatever is necessary" for the good of the other person or for the relationship. Over the course of our life together we may find that our commitment to one another involves us in situations that we never would have been able to predict on our wedding day. And yet we sense that this openness to "whatever is necessary" is at the core of the relationship that is our marriage for a lifetime.

Being a parent is another instance of diffuse and broad obligation. In becoming parents we commit ourselves to a range of responsibilities that we cannot fully predict ahead of time. We may have a sense of some of the emotional and financial resources that are necessary, but we cannot know for sure just what our own children's development will require of us. Will our baby be healthy or sickly, cranky or good-tempered? In school, will she be bright or slow, athletic or artistic, sociable or reserved? We cannot fully know or control these factors beforehand and yet we know that they will influence the shape of our responsibilities as parents.

Close friendship usually includes a sense of diffuse obligation as well, but with a greater expectation of mutuality than is the case between a parent and a growing child. My friend and I are not likely to sit down ahead of time and list the "rights and duties" that come with our being friends. It is more probable that as our relation grows we come to sense more concretely what we each can expect to give and receive in our friendship. And as the relationship grows, so may the sense of mutual obligation.

In many group settings the obligations that exist among members or between the group and an individual member are somewhat limited. Often these limits are specified explicitly in a contract or other legally binding form. The employees' handbook issued by many companies, for example, attempts to set out clearly the extent of the company's obligations to its employees (often expressed in terms of salary categories and fringe benefits) as well as the employees' obligations of presence and productivity to the company. Other aspects of employees' lives, other needs they may experience, are—strictly speaking—beyond the scope of mutual obligation that exists between employer and employee.

There are group situations that involve a range of obligations more limited than those diffuse responsibilities of marriage and close friendship, but in which many definitions of mutual responsibility remain largely implicit. That is not to say that these obligations are necessarily unclear. It may be very clear among the members of a diocesan religious education resource team (even though it does not appear in the bylaws) that, in a pinch, it is acceptable to ask for the loan of another member's car, but that it is inappropriate to ask for a loan of money.

There are instances today of efforts to clarify and make more explicit the range of obligation in some relationships traditionally characterized by diffuse mutual responsibilities. Some contemporary couples draw up marriage contracts that specify their sense of obligation to each other regarding finances, property, children, career, employment, travel, leisure time, provisions to be made in the event of death or divorce. Recent developments in religious congregations offer another instance of this move from diffuse to specific obligation. Formerly, the event of taking final vows, following upon a probationary period of several years, signaled the religious congregation's assumption of final responsibility for the individual member. The religious in final vows could feel confident that the congregation would provide "whatever is necessary," including—but not limited to—food and clothing, education, a place to work and a group with which to live, medical care—even long-term maintenance in case of illness or debilitating old age.

In religious congregations today there is a move from this broad and diffuse range of obligations to a somewhat more limited and considerably more specified set of mutual obligations. Thus the current documents of many congregations include explicit guidelines concerning the obligations that exist between congregation and member in regard to salary, job placement, living arrangement, the funding of education, preparation for retirement. For some, this move from a diffuse sense of mutual obligation toward a more specific statement of mutual responsibilities can be disturbing; it may challenge, perhaps even contradict, an earlier rhetoric and experience of the congregation as "my family." This change need not mean a deterioration of the mutual commitment, in either the psychological or the juridical sense, between the religious and the congregation. However its psychological and practical repercussions are significant enough to merit ongoing discussion within religious congregations. We may especially need to complement these moves clarifying the extent of our formal obligations with moves reinforcing and celebrating our sense of mutual commitment.

## How Are Group Members Evaluated?

Another important dimension along which groups may be compared concerns criteria of evaluation. What is the basis upon which the worth of an individual member is determined? In some groups a member is valued as a result of membership itself: a person is important to the group simply because she belongs, the basis of a person's worth is that he is "one of us." Loyalty among members is a significant expectation in groups of this kind. Family relationships give examples of this kind of loyalty. The family prepares for

Thanksgiving with the realization that "We have to invite Uncle Charlie." Nobody really likes Uncle Charlie. He talks too loud, he drinks too much, he even frightens the children. But he *is* Uncle Charlie—a part of our family. For better or for worse, he is "one of us." He belongs here with us, at least at Thanksgiving dinner.

There are other groups in which my value to the group is determined largely by my performance. The good group member is he who fulfills well the requirements of his role, she who makes an effective contribution to the group's task. And the better a person's performance, the more valued that person is. The more a group is involved in a task or a goal beyond the group itself, the more importance is likely to be attached to effectiveness and performance. I am likely to be valued in the planning committee to the extent that I can contribute to the plan. The neighborhood crisis center needs volunteers who can deal with troubled teenagers; the more effective I am with these young people, the more the center staff appreciates my participation in the volunteer program.

Many other groups fall between these two types—groups in which both "belonging" and "performance" are used to evaluate members. Sometimes one of these criteria will clearly be more important than the other ("I don't care what her ethnic background is, she does such a good job around here we ought to bring her into the management team"); sometimes one will be used to mitigate the effects of the other ("I know his sales quota is down again; but he's been with us since the beginning and we should take that into consideration"); sometimes the two are in clear conflict ("Sister Agnes is not a good principal for this kind of school, but she is a member of our congregation. Shall we keep her in that position, since she is one of us—or shall we give up this important position to a more effective 'outsider'?").

Throughout this discussion of the basic aspects of group life it has been noted that each dimension describes not a set of opposing categories into which groups will fall neatly, but a continuum along which groups will range. These dimensions provide an analytic framework for the minister's observation of those underlying realities of group life that are part of any effort at community formation. These dimensions can be recast as a chart and used to examine those particular groups with which my own ministry is concerned.

**Figure 3.1**

| DIMENSIONS OF GROUP LIFE* | Primary Group | 4 | 3 | 2 | 1 | 2 | 3 | 4 | Formal Organization |
|---|---|---|---|---|---|---|---|---|---|
| A. Primary focus of the group | Internal (group itself) | 4 | 3 | 2 | 1 | 2 | 3 | 4 | External (task or function) |
| B. "How much" of the individual is involved | Total (many aspects of self shared) | 4 | 3 | 2 | 1 | 2 | 3 | 4 | Partial (involvement limited to a particular role) |
| C. Degree of emotional exchange | Emotional Depth (sharing emotions is appropriate and necessary) | 4 | 3 | 2 | 1 | 2 | 3 | 4 | Emotional Neutrality (sharing emotions is inappropriate) |
| D. Basis for regulating behavior | Custom/Social Pressure (influence of tradition; common understandings) | 4 | 3 | 2 | 1 | 2 | 3 | 4 | Law/Contract/Procedure (explicit rules, norms, laws) |
| E. Scope of obligation among members | Diffuse (whatever is needed; loyalty) | 4 | 3 | 2 | 1 | 2 | 3 | 4 | Specific (limited by terms of a contract) |
| F. Basis for evaluation of worth of individual member | Ascription ("one of us," belonging to group) | 4 | 3 | 2 | 1 | 2 | 3 | 4 | Achievement (fulfills tasks or roles; evaluated on the basis of performance) |

*We wish to acknowledge the contributions of our colleagues Gordon Myers and James Zullo to the clarification of the chart.

The chart can be used to clarify my awareness of how a particular group is functioning currently or to objectify expectations of how this group could—or should—perform. As I use the chart I must of course remember that the judgment of where a particular group falls along the range of any of the dimensions may well differ from observer to observer. This judgment will surely differ from point to point in the history of the group's life.

The more a particular group is described at the left of the chart, the more it can be understood as functioning according to norms of primary groups, where priority is given to the group itself and to its maintenance and social cohesion. The more a group falls to the right of the chart, the more it incorporates elements of formal associations. Here there is likely to be a premium on effective performance and on the achievement of a corporate task beyond the group itself. This anlaysis of the elements common to all group life serves as a context for our consideration, in the next chapter, of the characteristics of community.

## FOR FURTHER REFLECTION

The dimensions of group life that we have discussed in this chapter can be explored in several ways. In the exercises below we suggest four directions in which an analysis may be taken. The questions may be used to clarify your own sense of how a group is functioning now (Exercise 1). Figure 3.1 can chart your awareness of how other members see the group (Exercise 2). Or you can use it to highlight changes (Exercise 3) or to point to problem areas (Exercise 4).

It is not necessary—it may not even be helpful—to reflect on all these at any one time. Instead, start with the first exercise, planning to take the time you need to respond and then to reflect on the information that emerges from your response. Plan to go on to the other parts of the reflection later, as your time and interest permit.

1. Select a group to which you belong and consider it in terms of the six dimensions of group life. Ask yourself the questions that appear on p. 34 and mark your responses along the chart on p. 45. As you reflect on the profile of the group that emerges, are you surprised by any of the judgments you made?

2. Now mark the chart as you judge most other members of the group would evaluate it. Compare with your own response. How do the two charts differ? What does this tell you about your own participation in the group?

3. Mark the chart to indicate the way you saw the group when you first began to participate in it. Again, compare this with your current evaluation. Are there significant differences between the two? If yes, why do you think this is so? Has the group actually changed? Have the changes been chiefly in your own awareness?

4. Mark the chart to indicate the way you would prefer the group to function. Are there differences between this "ideal" and the way you see the group as it actually performs? In what area does the discrepancy appear?

It can be useful for members of a group to undertake this exercise together. Have each member complete the chart, as suggested in 1 above and then discuss with other group members the similarities and differences that appear in their charts. The group may then wish to use the chart in one or more of the other ways suggested in this exercise, taking time after each personal analysis for some discussion of similarities and differences.


## ADDITIONAL RESOURCES

Over the past decade several significant discussions of community have appeared in religious journals with an international readership. Important among these have been: "Cultures and Communities," *Lumen Vitae* 32 (1977): 143–227; "New Forms of Community," *IDOC-International*, North American Edition (March 25, 1972): 2—70; "Community and Privacy," *Humanitas* 11 (1975): 5–113; "The Church as Communion," *Jurist* 35 (1976): 4–245.

Beginning in the mid-1970s the Christian Brothers have convened an annual interdisciplinary seminar involving about a dozen of their members in reflection on topics of significance to vowed religious life today. The papers prepared on each topic are published together in seminar reports available through the Christian Brothers' National Office (100 DeLaSalle Drive, Lockport, IL 60441). Several of these reports are relevant to the questions of group life treated in this chapter; see, for example, *Life Together: A Study of Religious Association* and *Power and Authority*.

The Alban Institute (Mt. St. Albans, Washington, D.C. 20016) is an ongoing source of quality books and pamphlets taking up a range of issues touching group life in the Church today. With a goal of making the best in the behavioral and organizational disciplines available to the Church, these brief and readable publications focus on questions of ministry and spirituality, the dynamics of parish life, and clergy-laity relationships. Its newsletter, *Action Information*, is an excellent introduction to the work and resources of the Institute.

*Parish Ministry* is the bimonthly publication of the Parish Project (299 Elizabeth Street, New York, NY 10012), sponsored by the National Conference of Catholic Bishops. Each issue includes brief thoughtful essays on parish life along with standard features treating parish staff, spirituality, and a review of recent resources. In *The Practical Guide for Parish Councils* (Mystic, CT: Twenty-third Publications, 1980) William J. Rademacher continues his long-standing contribution to the understanding and development of effective parish councils in Catholic congregations. Joseph M. Champlin, in his characteristically practical style, discusses parish community in *The Living Parish* (Notre Dame,IN: Ave Maria Press, 1977).

# 4 ✤
# Characteristics of Community

There is a basis for community whenever people discover that they share a concern for some significant aspect of their lives. If this common interest is important enough, it will move them to find opportunities to come together—to discuss, to plan, to act in common in light of these concerns. Community is begun in this context of communication and commitment to common goals. But it cannot persist long without an active appreciation for diversity within the group and a willingness to face and resolve the conflicts inevitable in any sustained human relationship.

In Chapter 2 we introduced the understanding of community as an intermediate style of group life. Groups that are communities operate neither simply as primary groups nor exclusively as formal organizations; instead, they function in ways that fall between these two styles. In Chapter 3 we looked at some of the elements that are a part of every group. We saw that there are differences among groups in regard to these issues and that some of these differences can be understood to range along the continuum extending from primary groups to more formal organizations. So if we were to use the diagram on page 45 to chart these questions, we would expect that in a group functioning as a community the responses would cluster toward the middle, with markings at *2* and *3* being much more likely than at *4*.

In this chapter we will continue the discussion of community as an intermediate style of group life. Our goal will be to fill out our understanding of this intermediate style, seeing it not simply in terms of what it is *not* (neither a *primary group* nor a *formal organization*) but in terms of its own particular characteristics.

Within the sociological discussion there emerge five character-istics of groups that function as communities. As a social style, a community is a group characterized by:

1. A common orientation toward some significant aspect of life;
2. some agreement about values;
3. a commitment to common goals;
4. opportunities for personal exchange;
5. agreed-upon definitions of what is expected of membership in this group.

### Common Orientation Toward What Is Significant

Community involves a common orientation toward some sig-nificant aspect of life. The ongoing patterns of interaction and com-mitment that are necessary for community cannot be sustained over trivialities. Community happens around matters of impor-tance. And since there are crucial differences among people in regard to what is important to them, it is useful to recognize that different people will move toward community around different issues. What is important enough to me to provide the enthusiasm and energy to work out the many complications of being together over time with a group of other persons may not be nearly so important to you. There are many persons, for instance, in our parishes and neighborhoods for whom religious faith is of such significance in their lives that it may well serve as a focus of com-munity for them. God, Jesus Christ, the Spirit, Christianity, the Kingdom, Church—these matter to them. Our ministries within the local parish are challenged to work creatively to assist the formation and nourishment of communities of faith among such believers.

But there are many people in our nation—and a good number in our parishes as they are currently constituted—for whom formal religion is not an important enough aspect of their lives to serve as a realistic focus of community. This comment can, of course, lead into a much larger discussion: what definition of religion is being used? should religion, however defined, offer the possibility of community for most people? whose responsibility is it if it does not? These questions, though significant, are not to the point of the discussion here. One reason it is difficult to build communities of faith in our parishes may well be due to factors of size or distance or the complexities of modern life. But another reason may be that parish ministers have inappropriate expectations that regular participation in the activities and programs of the local church should be of centrally compelling interest for large numbers of our fellow citizens. This simply is not the case.

But there are other facets of life which might serve as bases for community. For example, questions of childbearing and childrearing are, for many couples today, issues of great significance. Whether to have a child, if so, what patterns of love and discipline, of presence and absence, of "mothering" and "fathering" should be developed? Couples and, increasingly, single parents face these questions as issues of personal choice. Many such parents would respond well to opportunities to share their concerns, to discuss the dilemmas and delights of parenting that they experience, to discover and weigh—in an atmosphere of support and accountability—the options that are open to them. A group of these adults formed around a common orientation or shared concern for parenting would be likely to develop toward a social form of community.

There are other aspects of life that may serve as the focus of community—interest in the arts, commitment to social justice, appreciation of one's cultural heritage, concern for nature and the environment. Not all these concerns would provide a basis of community for everyone. Only that which is of significance in my own life can function as the foundation for my efforts to participate communally with others. Not all these concerns would lead, necessarily or explicitly, to the formation of a community of faith. But efforts at religious community that are not grounded in issues of vital personal significance to the members will be short-lived and superficial.

**Some Agreement About Values**

The importance to community formation of a common orientation or shared perspective leads to a second characteristic of those groups that function as communities. Among members of a community *some* agreement about values is likely—even necessary. It is often not enough that there be agreement that, for example, parents play a critical role in the development of their children. Those who are diametrically opposed about how parents should undertake to play that role—whether, for example, "children should be seen but not heard" or "children should be treated as equals in the family"—are not likely to function well together in a group organized around the values of parenting. They may, of course, work together quite well in some other situation. In a group concerned with the preservation of a common ethnic heritage, for example, they may find their values are more complementary.

A community, then, is a group characterized by some *agreement* (but only *some* agreement) about values. As a social form, community need not require total conformity on value questions. In a group that is functioning communally there is likely to be a good deal of congruence on values. Members of a community will tend to evaluate issues—especially issues that are central to the purpose of the group—in similar fashion. But the overlap will seldom be complete. There will remain areas, even areas of importance, where group members will differ. The group's future will depend in part on the members' ability to accept and harmonize these differences in ways that contribute to rather than detract from their life together.

The question of shared values can be especially volatile in the parish or other religious community today. The Church is in a time of staggering cultural transition, which has resulted in wide divisions within a hitherto more obviously unified body of Christian believers. For a religious group to function as a community there must be a sense that there are broad areas of agreement among members concerning the basic values of their religious experience. There are parishes today in which such a sense of congruence is lacking, parishes that seem polarized over questions of religious values and practice. Some religious congregations find themselves in a similar state. Efforts to enable these groups to experience themselves as a community of faith must involve explicit attention to this value gap. An approach that begins with the attempt to mask differences ("we are really all saying the same thing") or to legislate the end of polarization through enforced uniformity (either "liberal" or "conservative") is likely to miscarry. It is true that in many instances the value disagreements may be more apparent than real, more semantic than substantial. It is true that a leader may be called upon to take a stand in the controversy. But more central to the healing process is the attitude toward diversity and conflict that is displayed. A community's ability to move through its polarization toward a more mature expression of its shared belief will in many instances depend upon an experience of reconciliation. Ministers who manifest an appreciation of the range of values within the group and a patient confidence in the larger unity in which this value diversity is situated model an attitude that contributes to such reconciliation.

### Commitment to Common Goals

A related third characteristic of groups that function in the social style of a community is a commitment to common goals. Communities, more than primary groups, include a focus of concern that goes beyond the group itself. Within groups that function communally there is likely to be an interest in—even an enthusiasm for—action that flows from the members' common orientation and expresses their shared values. Members of communities are drawn to act together in the pursuit of those shared goals and ideals.

The parish, for example, is a community for action. Persons come together in the parish in order to accomplish, in ways they could not alone, their goals of worship and service. If it becomes difficult or impossible to accomplish my religious purposes in the parish— if, for example, parish organizations seem too outmoded to serve as the vehicle of my religious commitment to justice, or recent liturgical changes seem too great to permit my expression of worship—my commitment to membership and to participation in the parish can be undermined seriously. A parish community is not likely to develop without significant common goals; it is not likely to endure without effective common action.

In many religious congregations today the "problem" of community concerns this sense of common purpose or shared goals. Our corporate goals were clear, we may feel, when we all worked in institutions staffed by members of our congregation. What sense of shared purpose unites us now, we wonder, when we are involved in so many different kinds of work, sometimes working alone, often not under any explicitly "religious" auspices? If our sense of community is to survive these dramatic shifts in ministry, we will need to give special attention to the ways we experience and express our goals of common purpose.

Common orientation, congruent values, shared goals—there is

an important intellectual quality to these facets of the phenomenon of community. These characteristics remind us that community involves knowledge as well as love. Community invites its participants to shared activities of evaluation and planning as well as common actions of acceptance and support.

**Opportunities for Personal Sharing**
A fourth characteristic of groups which are communities is the opportunity for personal sharing. A group that intends to function as a community must build into the pattern of its life opportunities for members to communicate with each other at a personal level and to share expressions of mutual concern and care. It is important to remember here that there are many ways in which this can be done.

Communities involve "more" of members than do some other kinds of groups, but participating together in a community does not necessarily mean becoming close personal friends. Different communities will have different expectations about personal sharing—both *what parts* of our lives we share with one another and *how* we demonstrate to each other our care and concern. For example, though both groups may function as communities, the level of sharing in a priests' support group is likely to be different from that among the executive committee of the parish council. A prayer group probably has different expectations about mutual support than does the staff of a religious education office—but in both groups mutual support may be important. There are many ways, then, in which the gift of personal concern is offered and received. The challenge to ministers of Christian community is to be sensitive in supporting the expressions of personal sharing and concern appropriate to a particular group.

The development of these appropriate patterns of personal communication should not be left simply to chance. It is possible to overdo a group's concentration on its internal communication. But most groups err in the other direction—neglecting to develop and nurture opportunities for members to share with one another at both intellectual and extra-rational levels. Honest and direct communication among members is essential in a community: later in this book we will examine the attitudes and behaviors that contribute to effective communication. But equally and often even more important to the quality of mutual exchange in community is the opportunity for celebration, both in the sense of ritual and of recreation. Our community rituals—shared prayer and commemorative events and party festivities—engage us at a level that goes beyond our formal goals and explicit purposes. Often these moments of celebration include a sense of communion and solidarity among us. This enhanced awareness of our unity (community in the psychological sense) contributes significantly to the more ordinary processes by which we attempt to work out our ongoing relationships within the group (community in the sociological sense).

As we have mentioned before, the self-disclosure of deep friendship is not a necessary norm of personal exchange in every community. But in every community some appropriate and generally satisfying pattern of personal exchange must exist. Groups that do not give attention to the quality of mutual exchange and do not give time to activities of mutual support will not long survive as communities.

**Agreed-Upon Definitions**
A final characteristic of groups which are communities is the members' agreement about definitions and their shared expectations about how the group operates. Members need to know how the tasks of the community are divided up and what is expected of them and of others in regard to these tasks. Clarity about the group's patterns of leadership and authority is particularly important. This clarity and consistency involves (1) common understandings of the responsibilities that an individual assumes by becoming a member of this community, as well as (2) common understandings of how the various responsibilities within the group are related to one another.

Each of the five characteristics of community discussed here is an important, even essential, ingredient of any group that hopes to promote the experience of community among its members. But in the experience of many people, problems regarding mutual expectations are among the most troublesome obstacles to community. All of us are likely to have our own definitions of what constitutes an active parish, a successful parish council, a dedicated ministry team, a model religious house. Each of us carries, at least implicitly, a sense of what *should* go on within these groups and the others to which we belong. Our expectations serve as guidelines, influencing our own behavior and offering us criteria by which to judge ourselves and others. Complications can arise when we attempt to live together, to work together, to share our experience of faith—with each of us holding slightly different images and ideals of sharing, cooperation, authority, leadership. The diversity itself is not the problem. As has been suggested earlier, diversity—within certain wide margins—is a potential resource for community. Frequently, however, the problem is that these differences are not acknowledged and appreciated.

Let's take an example. For you, community means that as members of the same congregation we turn to each other first for support and companionship. The ministry that we do together is important to you, but you see it as a result rather than a source of our deeper communion. For me, community means that we are both motivated in our work by the strong religious ideal that the poor have the gospel preached to them. I care about you as a member of my congregation and I respect you as a dedicated minister, but I do not expect us to become close friends. Our differing expectations of community are not, of themselves, a problem. If we are each aware of what we expect in community and if we can make these expectations clear to one another early in our relationship, it is likely that we can come to some mutually satisfying understanding of what we can realistically expect of one another (and ourselves) in our community life this year. Over the course of the year we may each find that our own understanding of community has been enlarged by the other's point of view. Or we may realize that our differences are substantial enough that we are not able to undertake together the significant goals of shared community life. But in either case, this clarification has served our hopes for community.

When differences in expectation are not acknowledged they do not, for that fact, go away. Often they remain just below the surface—until such time as they erupt, now not as negotiable or even useful differences, but as irresolvable points of divergence and conflict. For example, having gone for several weeks or months on the assumption that "we all want the same thing" in our team meetings, we can become distressed as we begin to sense that this is not so. For you, the goal of the team meeting is to assure that the multiple responsibilities of ministry in this parish are assigned and carried out. You are convinced, however, that the demands of both ministry and personal maturity require that we function autonomously as we accomplish our tasks. But I am convinced that any "real" team must include at least group discussion and consensus decision-making; often there should be some coordinated action as well. I resist your attempts to streamline our meetings by delegating responsibility quickly and leaving individual team members to make their own decisions concerning their ministry. I begin to see your style as abrupt and even manipulative. You, in turn, are likely to interpret my resistance as disruptive of team ministry and as an attack on your leadership.

The conflict that often becomes inevitable at this point may serve the team well. The antagonism may help clarify some of the different possibilities for team functioning. Out of the ensuing controversy the whole team may be able to come to a better understanding of who we are and how we want to be together in our ministry. But often conflict does not have this good effect. Rather than seeing the controversy as a sign that there are differing expectations here that need to be clarified, many of us are more likely to respond to the emotional force of the argument, interpreting it simply as a clash of personalities or seeing it as an indication that the team is doomed.

Conflict is a powerful and often confusing dynamic in community; later in this book we shall discuss at greater length the contribution of both conflict and effective conflict resolution to community life. But here it is important to note several things: First, *some* conflict is expected and even valuable in the life of a flourishing community; it is not the goal of community life to do away with or deny all conflict among members. Second, not *all* conflict in groups is inevitable or useful; some kinds of dissention can lead to the disintegration of a group or, at least, of its effectiveness. Third, one of the ways in which a group can attempt to deal effectively with conflict is through its efforts of clarification.

The process of clarification, then, is central to community. It is an ongoing requirement, important not only at the outset of a group but as a continuing part of group life. Groups are wise to devote time during the initial formative stages of their life together to discussion of the hopes and intentions of the members, the roles and responsibilities that each will undertake, the patterns of authority and communication that shall prevail. But change and development are as much a factor in group experience as in personal life. Unless the process of clarification is continued, regularly or periodically, it is difficult to remain alert to the changing images, expectations, and needs that occur in the life of a community.

## The Ministry of Clarification

Throughout our discussion of community we have returned often to the themes of diversity and pluralism. Pluralism, we have maintained, can be an important resource for community. But it can be experienced, as well, as a source of complication and as a cause of confusion. The realization of this ambiguous function of diversity in the life of communities calls for a further comment on the ministry of clarification. The effort of clarification is an important initial step in the formation of a community of faith. This ministry of clarification can take several forms. First, there is the necessity to make explicit the "oughts" and "shoulds" that we use to evaluate ourselves and others in community. Often these value criteria upon which our judgments are based remain implicit, not fully available to ourselves or to others. This is not to suggest that these implicit personal standards are invalid. It is rather to note that when these criteria remain implicit and solely personal, misunderstanding and frustration can result.

Second, the sociological categories we have examined can themselves be used as tools of clarification. Let us take the analysis of the basic dimensions of group life in Chapter 3 as an example. An awareness of these dimensions can sensitize us to the role of these elements in our own group, whether this be a parish, a ministry team, a religious house, or other community group. Examining a particular group in terms of these dimensions will often provide deeper understanding and sometimes even new information about the group. The six questions that guided the analysis can direct our attention to aspects of the group's life that are central to its functioning and thus important to any ministry of community formation. An examination of a community in terms of these categories can help us recognize the group's strengths and diagnose its weaknesses.

This examination of a community may be undertaken communally. Group members can be asked to consider these questions and to share their responses with each other. The chart of group dimensions can be used to help members objectify their own expectations and compare these with the experiences and needs of others in the group. Where attitudes of honesty and acceptance prevail, this discussion can highlight areas of agreement, disclose differences in expectation, and reveal issues of potential concern. This exercise can result in an agenda for action to be undertaken by the group to enhance its functioning as a community. In addition, many people report that the attempt to clarify their expectations and experiences of the group, with an opportunity to share this with other members, is itself a community-building event.

A third important area for clarification concerns the costs of community. Community is not free; the benefits of social cohesion and belonging are paid for in the coin of personal accommodation and compromise. Any relationship requires that I give up some areas of my own independence. This is the price I must pay if I seek the goal of interdependence. An early enthusiasm may mask these costs. We may initially experience only the benefits of community—support, inclusion, communion, shared goals. But these real benefits cannot be sustained long in a group whose members do not have a capacity for generous self-disregard. Participation in community should not require me to annihilate myself or to give up all personal responsibility. But I can expect that participation in community will make real demands on me. It is important both for myself and for the group that we understand the costs that characterize our community. These costs differ from group to group. There will be differences within a group as well: a compromise that is acceptable to you may seem an unreasonable demand to me. The recognition of these differences does not, of itself, resolve them. We will need to go beyond clarification in efforts to negotiate, to come to a mutually acceptable resolution of the differences that exist. But here, again, clarification is an indispensable first step.

## A Vision of the Community of Faith

A vision of the community of faith emerges from our sociological analysis. We shall discuss it here using the parish as an instance. However, the vision is relevant to other expressions of religious community, as well.

The parish is the local body of believers whose religious hope is manifest in their ministries of service and sacrament. The parish most appropriately develops the social forms of community, since its goals include both an internal and an external focus. The parish is meant to nourish and express the communion that exists among its members; but this is a communion in meaning and mission as well as in fellowship. The experience of communion results from and is sustained by an awareness of shared meaning and a participation in the shared mission. The mission of the parish has a focus beyond the parish. The parish participates in the task of the whole Church—to witness to the world the saving presence of God among us.

For many, participation in a community of believers provides a larger social setting that assists them in mediating the claims of the conflicting value systems in which they are immersed through their daily life and work. In the religious community I can be reinforced in my struggle to establish and to maintain a sense of priorities that reflects my religious commitment. Such a community can serve as a context for personal integration, supporting the development of a life style in which my deepest values can be shared with others and expressed in common action. The community of faith is thus a social network in which people are challenged to personal conversion (values) and sustained in their attempts to live out the implications of this conversion (action). This personal transformation is the source from which committed religious action, or ministry, will flow.

In the end, the formation of the community of faith remains the work of the Spirit. A well-structured group that is clear in its goals, open in its communication, and committed to its religious values may still founder. Life remains that ambiguous; faith, that much a mystery. But the person who is aware of the social dynamics of group life and sensitive to the purpose and particular history of *this* group can contribute importantly to the possibility of community. And the possibility of community is the hope in which we stand, awaiting the gracious visitation of our God.

## FOR FURTHER REFLECTION

Use the five characteristics of community discussed in this chapter to reflect on groups in which you participate. Select a group that considers itself a community or functions as a community for you. Consider each of these questions in turn, taking time to allow yourself a full response. It may help to note down your comments as you go along, since you may find that you have more than one response to each question.

1. What is the significant area of life about which you are concerned in this group? Is there more than one area of significance?

2. What values do you, as members of the group, hold in common? Are there important values about which members differ? What are these? How important are these differences to the ongoing life of the group?

3. What are the goals and purposes of the group? In what ways do members act together to further these goals?

4. What are the patterns of communication among group members? When and how are members together in this group? What kind of personal sharing is encouraged? How satisfying are these patterns to you? to others?

5. Are individual members clear about what is expected of them in this group? Do members know what to expect from one another in the group? What are some of your expectations of "what is required" to belong to this community?

When you have completed these questions, look back over your responses. Do any of these areas seem to you to be "trouble spots" for the group? What actions might be taken to strengthen the group in each area?

## ADDITIONAL RESOURCES

The findings of recent research concerning small groups and larger organizations can provide insights to assist a ministry of clarification in the life of a community. In *Commitment and Community* (Cambridge, MA: Harvard University Press, 1973), Rosabeth Moss Kanter compares and contrasts the utopian movements of the nineteenth century in this country with the commune movement of the 1960s and 70s. The factors that she found to contribute to community formation and commitment have intriguing parallels in the structures of vowed religious life. Leland P. Bradford has edited *Group Development* (San Diego, CA: University Associates, 1978), a collection of essays discussing key factors that influence behavior in small groups. In *Systematic Helping* (Monterey, CA: Brooks/Cole, 1982) Gerard Egan offers a broad systemic model for assessing the current level of individual or group functioning and for planning effective change. Roy Lacoursiere examines the question of morale in the life of work teams and other collaborative groups in *The Life Cycle of Groups* (New York: Human Sciences Press, 1980).

The *Creative Leadership Series*, edited by Lyle E. Schaller for Abingdon Press and the *Creative Pastoral Care and Counseling Series*, edited for Fortress Press by Howard J. Clinebell, each include a number of excellent books, easy to read and practical in focus, which give additional tools for the ministry of clarification in church groups today. For a theological discussion intent on clarifying the role of ministry in the community of faith, see Bernard Cooke, *Ministry to Word and Sacraments* (Philadelphia: Fortress Press, 1975), Juan Luis Segundo, *The Community Called Church* (New York: Orbis Books, 1973), and Edward Schillebeeckx, *Ministry: Leadership in the Community of Jesus Christ* (New York: Crossroad Publishing Co., 1980).

# 5 ❊

# Community and the Larger Social World

To be in community is to belong. For many of us, it is this sense of belonging that most attracts us to community. We want to be part of a close-knit group in which sharing and emotional solidarity are strong. This is, at least in large part, what brings us together with others. And, as we have seen, experiences of solidarity and support are central in those styles of group life that are communities. But community is about more than solidarity and support. Communities are groups that have both an internal and an external focus. In communities we are concerned about what goes on among us *and* about the larger purposes that have brought us together. To concentrate solely on the internal aspects of community, on the experiences of belonging and support, is partial and often risky as well.

A heightened concern for support and belonging in community may reflect the absence of these experiences in the lives of many adults. Take friendship, for example—a relationship that offers much in terms of belonging and support. My friend is someone who knows me well, a person to whom I can reveal myself and who is open to me in return. Having a close friend with whom I can share confidences and upon whose affection and emotional support I can depend is one of the richest experiences of life. Psychologists are today beginning to affirm what many of us have already known—that a capacity for friendship is an important indicator of emotional maturity and that the presence of a close friend is a key factor in life satisfaction. With a friend I am both stronger and happier than without.

And yet I may sense that friendship is not frequent in my life. Many adults—perhaps even most—find that their mobility and the demanding responsibilities of their careers and families make it difficult for them to nurture close friendships. But without nurturing, friendship rarely flowers. Close friendship takes time. For most of us, the development of this kind of friendship requires some continuing contact, in an atmosphere that lets us feel secure in ourselves and safe with one another. But many of the situations that bring us together as adults do not offer such security. Within the dominant patterns of housing and work in the United States, many Americans sense their neighbors to be strangers and experience their coworkers as potential rivals. This sense of alienation from those we live near and work with makes it difficult for friendship to develop. We may be courteous and even sociable, but we are not likely to become close friends.

Friendship, if it happens for us at all, is more likely to happen "in private." In his influential report *The Seasons of a Man's Life*, for example, Daniel Levinson notes first that the experience of close friendship is rare in the lives of the men he studied and second that when a man in his study did speak of having a close friend, it was usually his wife that he mentioned. (It is probably equally important to note, however, that many men in this study did not experience their wives as also a "close friend.") It is likely that for a good number of American adults—both men and women, married and unmarried—friendship is, in Levinson's words, "largely noticeable by its absence."

If friendship, then, is rare, so also is a sense of effective participation in society. We may not really feel that we "belong" here either. Many people today do not feel "engaged" in the larger world of their own society. They are affected by developments in social and political life but feel powerless to influence these events. They are "patients"—those to whom things are done, not participants who act in and on the public realm. The sense that I am not really involved in the larger world of my own society can result in a sense of estrangement and alienation.

Such social alienation may be experienced as *normlessness* (I am not sure what to do, what is being asked of me, how I should act in the larger world), as *meaninglessness* (I have no sense of shared values; the goals and purposes that seem to motivate those around me are irrelevant to my own life), or as *powerlessness* (I am unable to control my own destiny; there is no way for me to influence the important events of my world). In contemporary life this sense of personal alienation is widespread. It is often experienced as a break between the worlds of my public and private life.

Enthusiasm for community as a source of belonging and support is related to this experience of alienation. For many, community is seen not as a way to become involved in the public world but as a refuge from it. The recent upsurge of interest in sects and cults can be traced in part to this desire for group support in the face of a confusing and even hostile social world.

This reclusive tendency in some groups has led persons who are concerned about public life and social action to be suspicious of community formation. They see the effort too often and too easily subverted into an almost exclusive concern for self-development or interaction within the group. Within the Church, for example, attempts to develop the more informal structures of prayer groups and experimental parishes have been criticized, often unfairly, as focusing too much energy on internal questions of group maintenance. Their critics point out that such self-absorption is scarcely compatible with the gospel's call to a mission of justice and mercy. Other people, looking at the experience of community organization and the "basic community" movement, see these intermediate groups as strengthening rather than distracting from public participation. The Church's experience in Latin America and elsewhere has shown that involvement in these communities can move an individual beyond a sense of isolation and impotence. These local communities of faith provide groupings in which personal values can be clarified and reinforced and in which joint action that is consistent with these values can be supported.

To understand community primarily as a sanctuary to which people can retreat from the difficulties of public life is to distort its goal and underestimate its power. Such an understanding compounds the underlying problem of alienation by reinforcing the break between public and private life. Worse, it distracts us from seeing communities as groups that can link individuals with society rather than shelter them from it.

## The Public and Private Worlds

The distinction between the public and the private realms figures significantly in our discussion here. While we have suggested that the radical split between public and private is a symptom of modern society, the distinction between these two areas of human activity has a long history. In the political theory of classical Greece, as social theorist Hannah Arendt has shown, the realms of public activity and private life were seen as sharply separate. Participation in public life, the highest function of citizenship in the city-state, was open only to adult men. Women and children, slaves and foreigners were excluded from this public world. Their words and actions were, by definition, part of the private realm only.

The Greeks, then, valued the public realm as an elite world of social discourse and civic action. Among them public life was seen as characterized by objectivity and pluralism. Public activity was behavior that could be seen and judged by others, each from a slightly different perspective within the common whole. The sense here is that what I do "in public" has a meaning that goes beyond just my own intentions. My public activities—my words, my works—stand on their own. They become part of a world that is bigger than just myself. Sometimes their effects may be quite different than I expect or intend. When I "go public" I enter a network of interaction that I cannot completely control.

In this classical view, private life—life in the family or household—is a "privation." While in this restricted sphere I am deprived of the experience of public life, deprived of those relationships that are seen to be necessary for the development of the adult (male) citizen's highest capacities for social discourse and shared meaning.

This early interpretation of "public" and "private" is alien to the way that many of us understand these terms today. Public life has fallen into disfavor among us; we find it difficult to appreciate the Greek enthusiasm for civic activity. It is even harder for us to sympathize with their apparently negative attitude toward private life. For most of us it is in the intimacy of our families that we find our deepest significance and satisfaction. It is not easy for us to imagine a participation in public life that would be equally nourishing.

In spite of, perhaps even because of, the differences between this classical view and our own, it can be useful to take a closer look at the Greek understanding. What, then, do they see as the "privations" of private life? In my private world I suffer the absence of a variety of other people. In my family or household I am not alone, but the range of social interaction in my private sphere is, by definition, limited. The private world is essentially the home of intimacy. Private relationships are strongly influenced by the factors of personal preference, affection, and individuality. These relationships are of crucial importance for my life, since they nurture my subjectivity and combat a debilitating sense of loneliness.

But within my private world I am without the social identity that comes from being seen and heard by those who are not my intimates. I am deprived of the objective relationship of being both engaged with and separated from a variety of other persons through the medium of a common world in which we all participate differently. In my private world I may feel deprived of an important experience of social achievement. What is done "in private" often remains without public significance or recognition.

Among the Greeks, it was largely women who suffered these "privations" of being excluded from the world of public activity. It may be useful to note here that many women feel these deprivations keenly today. They experience their adult lives as lived "in private," with their creativity and energy expended on tasks of family and home that are central to the private sphere but that increasingly seem to them without significance or value in the public arena. This does not mean that most women repudiate the private sphere. Rather they are becoming aware that the private realm is only part of life, only part of their own lives. They are choosing to complement their commitments in the private world with public roles and activities that place them more firmly in the web of a larger social reality.

**The Public and Private Worlds Today**

In contemporary experience the distinction between the public and the private realms has widened into antagonism. Specialization in modern society has brought more and more areas of life under the influence of the public realm. There are many ways in which we feel this public influence. To be a social worker or an accountant or a real estate agent in this state, for example, I probably have to function within a set of requirements concerning my training, the kinds of clients I can serve, the type of supervision I must have in my work. I am likely to feel that I personally have little to say about these requirements. I may sense that these official standards do not really reflect my own skills or the values I bring to my work, but I am bound by them nevertheless. As a teacher, I may have to pass periodic examinations if I am to retain my professional certification. My judgment may be that these tests have little to do with how good a teacher I am, but they remain a major factor in my career. Or I realize, as a homeowner, that the city's zoning laws have significant impact on the kinds of building that go on in our neighborhood. Yet the zoning board remains unresponsive to the concerns of families in our area. And all of us who are wage-earners are aware how much federal tax policy has to say about our use of money.

It is not political government alone that can have this "public" impact on our lives. Unions, professional associations, diocesan commissions—all these as well may function to regulate our behavior while they seemingly remain beyond our influence or direct involvement. Critical aspects, then, of my occupation, residence, finances, health, education are subject to government regulation or are controlled by other equally impersonal forces. These public forces may be experienced as unrelated to my own values and unaffected by my own agency. The public sphere then becomes increasingly anonymous and complex; it is unresponsive to my individuality and seems far removed from the influence of any choices I can make.

In its modern form private life can become, as social critics Peter Berger and Richard Neuhaus note, a "curious kind of preserve left over by the large institutions and in which individuals carry on a bewildering variety of activities with only fragile institutional support." The boundaries of this "left over" category, my private life, can seem to shrink until they encompass only those most limited areas in which I feel safe and in control. We can trace this movement of retreat from the public world.

### Retreat from the Public World

What am I good at? Where can I make a difference? Are there other people who care about the things that I think are really important? Can I make a contribution to more than "just me"? These are questions that, as I mature in competence and confidence through late adolescence into adult life, are likely to carry me beyond my circle of close relationships—my family and friends—into some participation in the larger world. But if my early efforts to participate in this larger world are unsuccessful—if I find no way for me to get involved; if what is important "out there" seems far removed from my own life or beyond the scope of my influence—then I am likely to pull back from this kind of public involvement.

A young manager comes to see that the fact that she is a woman will make it unlikely for her to be promoted soon to any position with real policymaking responsibilities. A political activist finds that his values of citizens' participation are irrelevant to the processes the party uses to select local candidates for public office. A black skilled worker begins to feel as much at odds with the white leadership of the union local as with management. In each case, the person's response may well include a retreat into private life.

If I feel unconnected from the larger world, then I do not look to that world as a place where I can make a contribution. If I sense that I must defend myself when I am in the public arena, then I am not likely to find much personal fulfillment in my public activities. The frustrations I experience in the social world may bring me back to my private world with heightened expectations. Here, among my intimates, I am safe. Here I am not anonymous. Here—and perhaps only here—can I "make a difference." It is here alone that I have any sense that my actions really count. It is not surprising, then, that I come to feel that personal meaning and fulfillment are to be found only in my private life.

But it is difficult to achieve meaning and fulfillment in the private realm alone. If my fulfillment can be achieved only "in private," it becomes increasingly likely that my attention will focus in on myself. As this happens, narcissistic images of success and satisfaction may begin to replace any larger sense of value and accomplishment. But if I look for fulfillment only in private, I am likely to be disappointed. The world of intimacy, as important as it is, is not the whole of life. It is difficult to come to a sense of personal competence and social identity in the private realm alone. This is, in part, because private life can seem so subjective. My own insights are important there and my personal preferences count, but I am left with a sense that I am very much on my own. Since my private world is so dependent on my personal convictions and transient feelings, I also know that it is not always reliable. I can come to experience my private world as unrelated to any larger social network of shared values or mutual obligations. Such networks of social obligation are, to be sure, constraints on my individuality, but they also help to root me in responsibility for my choices. And I sense that without some sense of social responsibility for my decisions and commitments, I am less than fully adult.

There is another reason why my pursuit of fulfillment exclusively within the limits of my private world is likely to be frustrated. The private world—a crucial context for my development through childhood and again in early adult life—normally needs to be transcended (though not repudiated) if I am to move into full maturity. One of the signs of adult maturity is an expansion of my capacity to care. As I mature, the boundaries of what really matters to me can be expected to widen to include more than just those things that directly touch my life. Increasingly I become aware that "my kind"—those who have some claim on my active concern and my resources—are not just my family and close friends. This sense of responsibility as an adult may lead to a personal investment in broader social issues: not just improving my child's school but working for a better educational system; not just keeping property values stable in our neighborhood but working for decent housing for low-income families in our city.

Signs of this maturity emerge in my concern for the well-being of a world that will outlive me. I am willing to get involved, to use my personal resources, to influence decisions that are being made now, in the hope that the future will be better—even though I sense that I may not live long enough to benefit from the results. It is enough that I can contribute, even if only in some small way, to a future that is better—for my children and my children's children, to be sure, but also for the children of the world.

The challenge to use my personal resources responsibly in the service of interests that go beyond myself is central to adult maturity. Private purposes and narrow individualism are not enough to carry me to this level of maturity. My circle of intimates may inspire and support my involvement in the larger world, but it is in the public world that my resources for this kind of generative participation are tested and strengthened.

But very often the public world does not seem open to my participation. It is an impersonal arena where the expression of values, purpose, and personal control may seems impossible or out of place. The "objectivity" of the public world can be a source of security—its demands are not likely to change from day to day or be subject to personal whim. But this objectivity is often experienced as alien. The public realm is not always related to the interests of the individual; it does not bend to human concern; it does not support personal goals.

One response to the harshness of the public world is to expand my investment in my private life. I start to spend more time on my hobbies or within my small circle of friends; I begin to focus my energy more exclusively on things that will benefit me and my loved ones directly. The difficulty in this approach, however, is that the sense of alienation cannot be overcome by retreat into a private world. That will only intensify the feeling of isolation from my culture. Social alienation can be overcome only by finding a way for me to participate in the public world.

**To Move Beyond Social Alienation**

Groups that are communities can help overcome this alienation. Communities, as we have seen, are intermediate forms of group life. Neither as private as a primary group nor as public as a formal organization, a community can offer a kind of "in-between" experience of what it is like to participate with other people. The people who can be with me in a community are not limited to just my intimates. There is more diversity, a greater range of interests, more breadth of purpose in a community than in a private household or among a circle of close friends. But a community is a richer context for relationships than is the public realm. In a community I can still sense that I "belong." My individuality is still important; I have something to contribute, not just in an anonymous role but because of who I am—my talents, my experience, my vision, my sensitivity.

A parish group may function as a community in this way. The members of the parish social ministry committee, for example, are not all close friends, but over the months they have been meeting they have begun to develop a sense of being committed to one another. Their early struggle to understand what kinds of concrete action they would take as a group has paid off. And while there are still times of confusion and disagreement in the meetings, most members now have a sense that their own contributions are valued and that they can count on others in the group to do their part as well. The group has not been successful in all the projects it has undertaken, but even the failures have been instructive. Belonging to a group has helped the members not to feel defeated. They have been able to support one another in some of the controversial issues they have dealt with; it has been reassuring for members to be able to depend on one another in projects that demanded a lot of work. Most members have commented that if they had had to do it alone, it is unlikely that they would have gotten involved at all. But being with a group, they felt the problems became more manageable. Coming together regularly also helped to keep their sense of commitment high.

Communities, then, can function as intermediate groupings, linking the public and private realms. In these kinds of groups my private life is expanded in a larger network of interpersonal commitments. In community I participate in a system of larger meaning and values that can help move me toward involvement in the public world.

Communities are intermediate forms of social life. The provincial team in a religious congregation, the adult education committee in the parish, a support group among professional women in the diocese, an ongoing task force of the priests' senate—groups such as these that function as communities have both an internal and an external focus, both a public and a private face. Because they occupy this intermediate space, they can play a mediating role, linking the person with the public world. They stand between individuals and the larger society, involving people in significant exchange with others who are not members of their smaller circle of intimates. Communities are social settings beyond the family, settings in which members can move beyond the psychological and social limitations implicit in private life into a middle ground of social interaction. Involvement in a community can challenge me to be concerned about issues that go beyond myself. Communities can help to focus this concern and to move it toward action. We shall discuss the role of community in action for social change in the next chapter.

**Community and Belonging**

Communities—as intermediate groups of shared value and purpose—can provide an antidote to alienation. They can expand our
sense of belonging, of "being at home" in the world. Groups that
function as communities invite their members to move beyond
both the security and the limits of intimate relationships, such as
bonds of family and close friendship, into a wider social realm.
But the social realm of community is more manageable than is the
complex and compartmentalized public world. The experience of
inclusion is important here. A characteristic of our own time is
that many people do not sense they belong in the public world. I
have to act in society, but I do so as a stranger. I may be a citizen
of this nation, a taxpayer in this city, a worker at this job—but in
all these transactions I often feel anonymous. It can be hard for
me to sense that who I am "in particular" makes any difference.
But if I feel included only in my family or among my intimate
friends, I am likely to experience the social scene—where I have
to act but do not really belong—as unsatisfying or even threatening.

A community is an intermediate grouping in which I can belong.
This belonging includes similarity and individuality. I sense that
these people are like me, perhaps not in every regard but in some
important ways. In addition, these people know me "in particular"
and value me as the particular person that I am. Here, to some
degree, I am special. I may not be unique, but at least I am not
merely a cog in a machine. I probably do not feel I am indispensable
to this community, but by the same token I realize that for these
people I could not be easily replaced by just anybody. To these
people I am important enough that when I am here I can be noticed
and when I am gone I can be missed. This is to belong. This experience of inclusion in a community is not the same as that experienced in family loyalties or deep friendship, but it is real. It
can be an experience of belonging in a context of pluralism. This
sense of belonging beyond the intimate relationships of my private
life can lead me to experience the public world in more positive
fashion. Being a part of a community can begin my movement
beyond alienation into a sense of being a part of and a participant
in my society.

Community is a setting that draws the individual beyond self
and intimates, beyond primary groups, toward roles of personal

agency and active investment in the larger world. In some groups this movement beyond intimacy is more obvious than in others. The faculty executive committee of the regional Catholic high school or the staff of a diocesan office of urban ministry may function together as a community. In groups like these the sense of common investment in larger social projects and public purposes can be high. But even in communities that include several elements of primary group style there is the invitation to move beyond private life. A support group among ministers or a small prayer group in a parish will generally include persons who are not one's close friends or family. My participation in these groups expands my network of social interaction. The personal and religious questions that are considered in these groups can broaden my focus beyond the boundaries of narrow self-concern. These settings, too, can invite me to get involved in purposes and projects that link me to the world beyond myself.

**Community and Shared Values**

Values are more than just personal convictions. They are one of the crucial points of contact between the person and the larger world of society. Disparity between my own values and those that are sought and appreciated in my society can contribute to the alienation we considered earlier. To sense that my values are just my own is disconcerting. If no one else cares about what I think is important, if no one else is moved by the things that motivate me, I can feel truly alone. I am left without a social context to reinforce my personal sense of meaning; I am left on my own.

Groups that function as communities can be contexts for social meaning. They can provide a larger-than-private confirmation of my values. My relationships with others in these kinds of groups can help me both to clarify my value commitments and to stay accountable to them.

Communities are groups of persons who have in common certain values and commitments. This sense of shared values contributes to a sense of social identity. I gain some sense of "who I am" from "what we believe." *I* stand for this because *we* stand for this. I belong to this "we": here I am supported and challenged to act on these values that we proclaim. By providing settings of value agreement and support, communities can moderate some of the strain that accompanies action in the larger social world. Community is a place where I feel connected to other people. Community can help move me beyond meaninglessness, helping me to realize that the values that give meaning to my life are not just my private affair. These values are held by other people, they make sense to others in the public world.

## Community and Shared Purpose

Communities link members with the larger social world by helping to overcome the sense of powerlessness. Communities are contexts of shared purpose as well as shared values. A community can lead me not only to clarify and commit myself to values, but to act on them—to construct a life style and to undertake activities that manifest in my behavior the significant values to which we are committed. Participating with other people in a community, I can come to a sense of what might be done, what action I might take or we might take together, on issues that are important. I can be supported in my attempt to undertake these actions. I can be encouraged to continue when the action is difficult or when results are not immediate or clear. In community I can be appreciated for my efforts, congratulated in my success, and accepted in my defeat.

One of the social strengths of groups that are communities is the possibility of joint action. For some groups this action may be focused primarily within the group. But most communities will be committed to some action beyond the group in pursuit of the values that mark the group.

There are expectable differences among communities in the ways that the group supports action. One group, for example, may inspire and support individual action: "The sisters with whom I live this year are all working in ministries different from my own, but the quality of our religious life together strengthens my personal commitment to my own work." In another community, a few members may act as representatives of the larger group: "The task of negotiating with the chancery representatives over the terms of the contract that the diocese offers to lay people seems easier for us, as officers of the Lay Ministers' Caucus, when we recall the growing sense of solidarity in our group on these issues." Or a group functioning as a community may plan and act together: "As an ecumenical team, we have decided to coordinate our various activities in campus ministry this year, to reflect a common set of priorities and to contribute to a joint pastoral goal."

The structures of community both challenge me to, and provide a vehicle for, greater public involvement. It is likely that the values or issues around which a community gathers are themselves connected to the public world. Commitment to community and its goals will challenge me to deal with this public world to influence it, perhaps to change it.

My community, then, can be a social setting in which to stand as I confront the larger issues and concerns of public life. Participating with others in community can assist my commitment to this larger world—by personalizing the issues involved, by helping me decide what can be done, by giving opportunities for collaborative action and personal support. Communities help me to come to a sense that there is something I can do and that I will not be alone as I do it.

Thus the social forms of community can play a mediating role in society. The structures of community offer a supportive context of smaller size and complexity that can serve as a bridge between the individual and the public world. The shared value context of a community can provide an experience of common meaning, enabling me to establish and maintain a set of personal values that are not simply idiosyncratic. A community can bring members to sense that action is possible. It can help members focus their action and can support them in it. A community can assist me to work out a set of personal priorities and help me sustain my commitment to the behavior and life-style that support these priorities. In these ways, groups that function as communities can serve as social settings in which and through which members can recognize and participate in a wider, public sector of life.

## FOR FURTHER REFLECTION

Consider your own experience of the private and the public realms.

1. What groups or relationships are chiefly a part of your private life? List the people who are with you in this way.
2. What groups or relationships in your life now do you understand to be part of the public world for you? Again, list these relationships and groups.

3. Does any group play a "mediating" role for you, providing a sense of belonging and at the same time assisting you to participate in the larger social world? How does this happen? What are the particular ways in which this group supports and challenges you beyond your private life?

4. Of the groups that you listed in your responses above, do you consider any of these a "community"? Why or why not?

## ADDITIONAL RESOURCES

Hannah Arendt has provided a valuable discussion of "The Public and the Private Realm" in Greek political thought in her book *The Human Condition* (Chicago: University of Chicago Press, 1958). Parker Palmer challenges religious groups to move beyond goals of intimacy in order to work more consciously as a force for the renewal of public life in his working paper *Going Public* (Washington, D.C.: Alban Institute, 1980) and in his expanded discussion, *The Company of Strangers: Christians and the Renewal of Public Life* (New York: Crossroad Publishing Co., 1981).

In their slim volume *To Empower People* (Washington, D.C.: American Enterprise Institute, 1977) sociologist Peter Berger and religious author Richard Neuhaus discuss "The Role of Mediating Structures in Public Policy." They include a consideration of the role of the Church as a mediating structure in American democracy. In *The Church Community: Leaven and Life-Style* (Notre Dame, IN: Ave Maria Press, 1973), Max Delepesse draws on his experience with an "intentional" Catholic community in Europe to show how Christian community can be a symbol not only of how Christians should live together but of how the mission of justice and mercy can be served. Paul L. Roy explores the dynamic of the faith-sharing experience that is at the heart of the movement of Christian Life Communities in *Building Christian Communities for Justice* (New York: Paulist Press, 1981).

# 6 ✤
# Other Possibilities in Community: Personal Integration And Social Change

Community is a style of social interaction with many possibilities. Not every community realizes all of these. Groups that are communities differ in what they wish to be for one another and what they wish to contribute beyond themselves. The sociological category of community, falling along the intermediate range of group styles, leaves room for much diversity. We have already discussed several results that are possible within groups that come together as communities: community can provide a sense of belonging; community can connect me with the larger world; community can enliven my commitments in faith. Here we will examine two other outcomes that are related to groups that function as communities: community as a context for personal integration and community as a vehicle of social change.

Again, the suggestion we make is not that every community *is* or *should be* concerned explicitly with these goals of personal integration or social change. Rather, we suggest that the patterns of belief and behavior that characterize communities (constituting their status as intermediate kinds of groups) are well suited to these goals. Those concerned with personal integration or involved with efforts of social change are likely to experience the group patterns of community as most supportive of their goals.

## Community and Integration

A community, as we have seen in Chapter 5, involves me beyond the close circle of intimates, but in such a way that "more" of me can come into play than is usually the case in my public life. In my community I can be known not just in a segmented way, not just in one isolated role, but more fully.

Many of the social roles of adult life are restricting in that they permit only a part of my personality to come into play. I sense, for example, that what I do as an assembly-line worker or a tax consultant or a grade school teacher is not "the whole me." Some roles are even more limiting in that they require that I hold in check, or even deny, important parts of who I am. For example, there are some roles in which my sense of humor must be downplayed; others where I must act to challenge my colleagues rather than to support them. Some of my responsibilities may require an almost exclusive focus on the logical aspects of problems, forcing me to overlook their emotional content. These restrictions may be appropriate for the job at hand. But in accepting these job-related restrictions on my behavior, I can expect to experience some strains. I may even, eventually, lose access to some parts of myself. This is especially likely if, as for many adults, I act in the public world chiefly through my work-related roles.

Participating in a community can help me stay in touch with this larger range of my own personality. In a group that functions as a community I can be known more fully than through the segmented and partial roles I play in the public world. The expanded social context which is community allows intellectual, emotional, and value aspects of the self to come into play. In community settings there is likely to be more room for parts of the personality that are necessarily—and perhaps even usefully—set aside in the dominant roles of one's adult responsibilities. For one person, community will call out emotional resources that are not legitimate in his work. For another, community may provide an opportunity for an intellectual contribution: here her ideas and plans and goals are appreciated. For others, interaction in community will be an important help in acknowledging and affirming the values that are important for them: "These people help me keep alive my vision of what is really important in life."

My participation in the public world often does not leave room for the clarification of my values on complex issues or for the expression of my emotional responses to what I experience. What is demanded of me, instead, is the "objective" and even "disinterested" stance of the noninvolved professional. I am required to put aside the larger issues and to exercise my skills in the immediate and more limited sphere of my direct responsibilities. A group that is a community can be a force for my personal integration by assisting me to clarify my values and to establish priorities that help me live out these value commitments. In my work place, for instance, I may sense that a culture of competition and materialism prevails. People are out to make money because money is the key to "the good life." I enjoy my work and I appreciate its financial benefits—but I want both my work and my money to be for more than "just me" and even just my family. But how do I keep these values alive, how do I hold myself accountable to them in the practical decisions I must make about career advancement or about how our family uses money? Involving myself with others who share my values and concerns can be one part of such personal accountability. In such a community I can come not only to a clearer awareness of what is really important to me but to the realization that these values are not simply idiosyncratic. Others see the world as I do; others share my own convictions about what really matters in life. The community context thus supports my commitment to values by reinforcing their validity at both the intellectual and emotional levels. These people can also help to hold me responsible for living my life according to what I believe, even when there are personal risks or financial costs involved.

Participating in a community can help me clarify my values; it can also help me to mediate conflicting role demands. Adult life involves each of us in a variety of roles—I am worker, friend, colleague, family member, citizen, and more. These different roles make differing and sometimes incompatible demands on me. My responsibility in my job may require that I bring work home over this weekend; my responsibilities as a friend or as a spouse may demand that I spend time this weekend with someone I love. It is often difficult to reconcile these obligations. If I attempt to meet all the role demands made on me, I can feel overwhelmed. I quickly sense that I do not have the resources—of time or energy or concern—to do all that is "expected" of me. But left to myself, it may be difficult for me to establish any sense of priority among these multiple demands. Here again, community can be a context of integration. With its milieu of support and shared values, a community can provide a setting in which I can sort out these demands and come to a responsible compromise. This kind of group can help me set my personal priorities in line with the higher values of my life and help me act according to these priorities. In community I can be supported to face the guilt or blame or social pressure that may accompany my decision to say no to some demands and to respond more selectively to others. Thus a group that functions as a community can help members move beyond an experience of internal conflict and fragmentation toward a more integrated sense of personal priorities.

One of the reasons that a community setting can be so useful in helping us sort out our priorities and stay responsible to our value commitments is its public face. Community, as an intermediate style of group interaction, takes us beyond the intimate space of our closest personal relationships, the domain of our private lives. Community is part of social involvement, it is an enlargement of private life. Dealing with my values in the more public setting of a community can help me carry these sometimes fragile convictions into my even more public behavior in the larger world of my work and social responsibilities.

Thus we have a movement beyond intimacy, but one which retains a human face. Community invites me into a manageable intermediate arena where I can act more "wholly"—beyond some of the limitations of role or objectivity that frequently accompany my public activity. It is also an arena of challenge, where honest communication is possible, where I can experience the benefits of both support and criticism, reinforcement and confrontation.

It is in this sense, then, that groups that function as communities can be contexts for personal integration. In a group that functions as a community I can experience myself (and be experienced by others) more completely and authentically, apart from the sometimes restricting demands of my social roles. In a community setting I am more likely to be free to express both emotional and intellectual aspects of myself. The supportive atmosphere and shared values of a community can help me to respond selectively to the expectations that arise in the course of my participation in the public realm. In such a community I can learn to discriminate among these demands and to establish priorities regarding the sometimes conflicting requirements of my adult roles.

## Community and Change

There is a tradition of analysis in the social sciences that sees community as a conservative force, reluctant to change. And in their personal experience as well, many people attest that the communities or groups to which they belong have held them back or presented obstacles to significant personal development. A young adult senses that many of her family and close friends do not want her to pursue the career for which she has demonstrated talent but instead are pressing her to marry soon and devote herself to a family. A member of a ministry team resents the caution of his colleagues, who urge him to "go slow" in his attempts to implement a policy of effective lay leadership in the parish. A woman religious is aware of the disapproval of her sisters as she develops friendships beyond the congregation. In each of these cases a group may be experienced as inhibiting personal growth.

But this is not the whole story of the relationship between community and change. Many of us who have experienced change in our personal lives know the importance of a supportive group. Whether the change we experience is the more obvious crisis of serious illness or emotional distress, or the sometimes disguised crisis of a job shift or a change in residence, we know we could not have made it through without the understanding and encouragement of our friends.

The connections between community and personal change are strong. Most religious traditions are aware of this: religious conversion is an act of the individual and involves significant personal transformation, but it is seldom achieved "alone." If this initial transformation is to mature into a new way of living, the neophyte must become a part of a community of believers; for it is in relations with these other believers that new and fragile faith is nurtured and strengthened. This communal dimension of conversion is strong in the new Rite of Christian Initiation for Adults, now an important part of the life of many Roman Catholic parishes.

If the connections between community and personal change are strong, so are those between community and social change. The movement of social change, whether through reform or revolution, includes groups of people held together by a sense of solidarity who are capable of acting together to achieve their goals. The labor movement, the civil rights movement, the women's movement, the peace movement, the pro-life movement—all of these efforts at social change found their earliest strength in groups of people who shared a vision of how things should be different and were willing to act together to affect that change.

## The Dynamics of Social Change

Elizabeth Janeway has explored this connection between community and social change in her recent book, *The Powers of the Weak*. Social power—the ability to influence outcomes and control resources—is not simply an attribute of those persons who are designated leaders, nor is it just a quality of the offices they hold. Social power is in good measure an element of a social relationship. Social power is something that *goes on between* those who govern and those who are governed. When this relationship is healthy, it is marked by reciprocity—each party has something to give to the relationship, each gets something from it, each has a sense of some control in how the relationship is going. The leader, for example, makes decisions, policies, and laws that achieve the goals of the governed and are oriented toward the "common good." The governed give legitimacy, the acceptance of the leader's right to govern.

This experience of reciprocity describes, in Janeway's terms, the ordered use of power, in which the leader acts with the consent of the governed. This ordered use of power can be threatened by leaders who cease to act for the common good. They may misjudge what is for our good (as we see it); they may be ineffective in achieving it; or they may start to use the resources of their position for personal privilege. When the relationship of social power is thus threatened, the response available to the governed is to withdraw legitimacy. In some settings this may be done by established peaceful means: in the next election, we vote this set of leaders out and a new set in. But this peaceful withdrawal of the consent of the governed is not always available. Those in power have many resources to help them stay there—even against the will of those over whom they exercise social power. The governed are seldom in a position to take away from the leaders the resources of power—whether these be wealth, military might, or control of needed resources. But they can begin to question what those in power are doing. This seems a fragile, perhaps even an illusory "power" of the governed—but it is here that change begins. I cease to accept that "the way things are" as defined by those in leadership roles is, in fact, how things are or how they should be. Most significantly, I refuse to accept their definition of who I am and how I should act. Options other than the status quo then become imaginable; this is the first step toward their becoming possible.

Social change, then, starts here. When the governed are able to question the legitimacy of their leaders, they themselves have begun to exercise power. The ability to "disbelieve" the way that the powerful have defined the situation that exists between us, the realization that their power over me is in part due to my acceptance of their right to rule—these changes in awareness mark a significant personal change. When many of us come together in this awareness, we can become a potent force for social change. Consciousness-raising efforts among women and other minority-status groups in the United States, conscientization projects among the poor and politically disenfranchised in Third World countries—in these and similar ways advocates of social development attempt to nurture this first and most basic dynamic of social change.

While this first "power of the weak" is not illusory (Janeway and other social analysts have documented the revolutionary effects of such a change of consciousness) it is often fragile, especially in its early stages. It is here that community becomes crucial. Finding others who share my new awareness helps that awareness to grow strong. Without this experience of shared vision or, at least, shared disbelief, I may be overwhelmed by this discrepancy I feel. It is hard to trust my own awareness when it begins to contradict what has until this time seemed normal and necessary, even to me. If I am alone, my growing suspicion that something is not right can begin to feel like "my problem." It is perhaps I who am troubled, not the situation.

But as I find that others share my concerns, I can begin to take my experience and my new awareness more seriously. Janeway sees this "coming together" as the second power of the weak. We come together, first, to feel connected and to give each other support in our new way of seeing the world. This solidarity is central to our confidence and sense of purpose But ultimately this sense of solidarity is not enough; as our trust of ourselves and one another grows, we are moved to act. Strong in our awareness that there are many of us, that we want the same things and that our goals are just, we organize ourselves to do something about what we believe.

We have come to the third power of the weak: positive action to achieve our own goals. Thus a movement for social change takes shape.

### Community in the Dynamics of Social Change

Let us explore some of the connections between this analysis of social change and our earlier discussions of community. To be an effective movement for change, the "coming together" of the governed must include both solidarity and positive action or, in our own terms, both belonging and purpose. Groups that are successful in achieving this dual focus are likely to develop patterns among themselves that are similar to those we have described as characteristic of intermediate social forms. Thus, if we are to undertake action for change, we must organize ourselves and our resources; this will involve our coming to some agreement about tasks and roles and responsibilities among us. But we cannot let these structures develop in a way that destroys our sense of shared vision or our experience of mutual support. Both solidarity and effectiveness remain priorities in our action. As a group we are concerned about both our life together and our success in changing the way things are "out there." This combination of both internal and external goals is, as we have seen, more characteristic of a community than of a primary group or formal organization. Thus, the rich and complicated set of goals that is held by groups intent on social change is more likely to be served by structures that fall along this intermediate range of those available to group life.

Not every community, to be sure, will be concerned with social change. But as a group form, community has the potential for serving the goals of both solidarity and effective group action that are basic to the sustained effort required for either revolution or reform.

### FOR FURTHER REFLECTION

Most of us have experienced both the positive and the negative influence of the groups to which we belong. One group helps me come to a deeper sense of personal integrity; another holds me back. In this community we come together effectively to plan and act for change; in another there is pressure to keep things the way they have "always" been, even when this way no longer works very well. Reflect now on your own experience of the ambiguous power of groups.

1. Consider the community experiences that have been important for you over the past several years. Take time to recall these various groups and how you were involved in each. It may help to take notes as you bring each group to mind.

2. Now look at the question of personal integration. First, consider what "personal integration" means to you. Be as concrete as you can, giving your own examples. Then look at the groups in your life. What positive contributions have these made to your sense of personal integration? Has any group had a negative influence? How?

3. Then turn to the question of social change. Have you been involved in group efforts for institutional change? Again, be as concrete as you can, giving your own examples. How have the groups in your life contributed to these efforts toward change? Have the groups in which you participate ever hindered your efforts at change?

## ADDITIONAL RESOURCES

In *Stages of Faith* (New York: Harper & Row, 1981) James Fowler touches on the significance of community as a context for personal integration, discussing the role of shared images and commitments in the development of a personal framework of meaning. The interaction between religiously inspired communities and personal integration is examined, from somewhat different perspectives, by Jean Vanier in *Community and Growth: Our Pilgrimage Together* (New York: Paulist Press, 1979) and Joseph Haroutunian in *God With Us: A Theology of Transpersonal Life* (Philadelphia: Westminster Press, 1980).

Dietrich Bonhoeffer has explored the relationship of faith and community in his important essay *Life Together* (New York: Harper & Row, 1976). Rosemary Haughton treats the connections among faith, conversion, and community in her classic, *The Transformation of Man* (Springfield, IL: Templegate, 1980).

Elizabeth Janeway draws insights from a variety of social science orientations in her examination of the dynamics of social change in *The Powers of the Weak* (New York: Alfred A. Knopf, 1980). The Inter-Religious Task Force for Social Analysis has developed a valuable study and action guide for religious groups confronting issues of social change in *Must We Choose Sides? Christian Commitment for the 1980's* (New York: Episcopal Church Publishing, 1979). In *Empowerment: Skills for Parish Social Action* (New York: Paulist Press, 1979) Harry Fagan provides practical strategies to serve the religious community in its efforts of social change. Charles Keating discusses planning as a tool of change in *The Pastoral Planning Book* (New York: Paulist Press, 1981).

# ✤ PART III

---

# FOSTERING CHRISTIAN DREAMS IN COMMUNITY

# 7 ✤

# Christian Community—
# Mediator of Dreams

How does a Christian community contribute to and shape the religious maturity of its members? A community of faith—a parish or a diocese or a religious congregation, for example—is not meant to be merely a passive arena in which individual Christians mature. Rather it has a central role to play in the ongoing process of conversion and transformation. A crucial function of a faith community is that of *traditioning*—handing on Christian hopes and values. In this activity a community of faith mediates its inherited values and its deepest convictions to its members. It hands on the Christian dream.

A dream, as Daniel Levinson has suggested in *The Seasons of a Man's Life* and as we have discussed further in *Christian Life Patterns,* can be understood as my life ambition, my deepest and best hopes for what my life can be. With this understanding, Christian formation can be seen to involve the intersection of three dreams. First, as individuals, our religious maturing involves the growth and purification of our dream—our vocation. Second, our personal hopes and ambitions arise in and are shaped by the dreams that are alive in our environment. The deepest hopes of our parents, the models we have in school, the vision alive in our parish—these influence our own dreaming in powerful ways, both for better and for worse. Each of us learns very early, by observing the Christians around us, what Christians live for and how they comport themselves in the world. But the dreams and religious hopes of a family and a parish do not exist alone. As Christian dreams, these group ambitions are finally shaped by a larger vision—the collective dream of believers, the kingdom of God. This dream, which is both the source and the goal of every Christian vocation, is our inheritance. When the faith of a community is lively, the community mediates this collective dream of the kingdom of God to its members. A community does this as it develops and purifies its own dream or vocation. We will explore how our religious maturing is shaped by this intersection of three dreams.

**Christian Vocation: The Maturing of a Dream**

It can be fruitful to explore the process of personal religious maturing in terms of the development of a dream. Following Daniel Levinson, we will understand a *dream* not as a sleeping fantasy, but as a *life ambition*—a gradually emerging and changing sense of what I might make of my life. The first hints of a life dream emerge in our childhood announcements of "what I want to be when I grow up." Our family and immediate environment provide the context of our life ambitions: the toys we play with, the way we are dressed, the interaction of our parents—all these provide the shape and boundaries of our future dreams.

Dreams and life ambitions are fragile parts of our childhood and adolescence; they can be easily lost or broken. Parenting is, in large part, the nurturing of dreams. For most of us, our parents transmitted the values and images that ignited our first dreams. They appreciated our hopes, recognized our strengths, supported our growing independence. In other ways—by neglect or by forcing their own life ambitions on their children—parents can negatively shape their future.

In late adolescence and early adulthood our dreams begin to be tested. In our first jobs and early adult relationships we tentatively try out our life ambitions, testing them against our own abilities and against the world of adult responsibility that we are entering. "Will it be possible, am I capable enough to pursue this career or hope?" As Levinson observes, much of the decade of one's twenties is likely to be taken up with this testing of the dream. We seek jobs that will give our dream expression; we search for groups of people who will support our still unsure hopes. Even when our life ambition finds expression in a satisfying career or personal commitment, we will need to return to this dream later in life as it matures and is purified.

The psychological maturing of an adult can thus be charted according to the growth of a dream: its emergence (or absence) in childhood; its tentative exploration in young adulthood; its reexamination in later years. For Christians this personal development takes place in the context of a faith community with its own values and dreams. Thus, the development of our personal dream is, in fact, the growth of a vocation.

*Vocation:* A Christian vocation is a calling, an invitation to do something special with my life. A vocation is a dream personalized: we are invited by God to pursue the powerful religious hopes we find within ourselves. We experience ourselves being led, called, or even coaxed to live our life a certain way.

*Vocation* does not refer only to a few life choices—such as a vocation of a diocesan priest or vowed religious. A vocation describes how each Christian is called. Each of us is called not by some external decree, but by the Christian values and hopes gradually taking shape within us. As these received values and convictions are shaped by our own developing abilities and gifts, our vocation begins to emerge. Thus, a vocation is not something we "should do," but is, in fact, *who we are,* trying to happen. A Christian vocation, like a dream, is a lifelong revelation of who we might be. In our vocations we are gradually revealed to ourselves. The specific shape of "who we might be" is not grounded in someone else's demands or values; it is grounded in our own abilities as these are formed by the Christian hopes that we most cherish. Naturally, then, a vocation cannot be fully realized at age twenty-one: we could not, at this young age, grasp the richness and complexity of who we are to be. Yet in our twenties we begin the journey of trying to realize our best Christian hopes in our commitments of love and work.

The idea of the dream seems especially suited to clarifying the growth of a religious vocation because these notions share many characteristics: each is a fragile, slowly developing life ambition, shaped by certain values; each is an exciting hope for our life, but often vague and in need of considerable attention; both arise from within us—though strangely independent of our planning and control—and mature over a lifetime.

In *Christian Life Patterns* and again in *Marrying Well* we have examined how the dream and vocation changes and matures in midlife. The accumulated experience of our thirties and forties will likely bring us to reexamine the course of our life. Often, in some special moment of grace (sometimes precipitated by a crisis in work or family life) we are invited by God to a purification of our dream. I may be asked to let go of illusions about myself that were once necessary but no longer serve me well. I may be invited to heal the more compulsive parts of my life ambitions that have driven me and those around me. I might be called to give attention to a dream long deferred or ignored. Important as these "reconciliations with the dream" are, we will not discuss them here. Rather, we will pursue the relationship between the growth of our personal dreams and the support of a faith community. Neither dreams nor vocations grow in isolation; each depends on environments where dreaming is nurtured, even as it is shaped, by certain values. In the following sections of this chapter we will examine the collective dream in which Christian values are communicated to individual believers and the way a faith community mediates this dream to its members.

## The Collective Dream of the Kingdom of God

The dreams of Jews and Christians are rooted in and formed by a dream that has been maturing for three thousand years and more.[1] Abraham sensed that he was being invited to leave his ancestors' home in search of a new land and a different way of life. In his dream of a different and exciting future our own religious ambitions were born. Hundreds of years later his descendants, having escaped from Egypt and now wandering in the Sinai desert, would remember this dream of Abraham. Was it not the same God who had called Abraham to his search who now impelled them to the dream of a secure and prosperous homeland? In the aridity of the desert this dream was pictured as "a land rich and broad, a land where milk and honey flows" (Ex. 3:8).

Three characteristics of this dream merit attention here. First, this was a collective vision, a life ambition that belonged to a group

1. Rudolf Schnackenburg provides a careful survey of Old Testament and New Testament understandings of the kingdom of God in *God's Rule and Kingdom* (New York: Herder & Herder, 1963). For a discussion of the appearances of the kingdom of God in the New Testament, see p. 79ff; for Schnackenburg's discussion of the different possible translations of the phrase *Basileia tou Theou*, see p. 354ff. Schnackenburg translates *Basileia* as the "reign" or "rule" of God to express the ongoing aspect of God's guidance of human life. "Kingdom of God" suggests to him a completed or realized state of affairs rather than this continuing presence and guidance. Others have challenged the translation of "kingdom of God" on the grounds of its quaint or medieval sound. What is needed, perhaps, is a contemporary metaphor to convey God's shaping influence in our personal and social lives now and in the future.

of people. Second, it was a dream received as a promise from someone they would come to call Yahweh; this dream was not their own invention, did not originate in them, but came from God. Third, however this dream would be interpreted, it would always draw this group of people out of the present toward a new and different future.

The vision of a land flowing with milk and honey seemed, at first, to be realized in the new land of Israel and the kingdom that David and Solomon ruled. But as social injustice and the abuse of power grew, as Israel's infidelities to Yahweh's covenant multiplied, it became clear that their collective dream was far from realized. It began to seem to some that the very greatness of their state and their kings was a distraction from this dream.

As Israel matured (through failure and conversion and more failure—the usual route of maturity), prophets appeared to reexcite the people to their collective dream and also to further nuance this hope. Isaiah and Jeremiah were especially insistent that this dream of an idyllic place "flowing with milk and honey" must also include care for the poor, the widowed, and even the stranger. Isaiah envisioned a society in which sacrifices are replaced by care and justice:

> *Take your wrongdoings out of my sight.*
> *Cease to do evil.*
> *Learn to do good,*
> *Search for justice,*
> *Help the oppressed,*
> *Be just to the orphan,*
> *Plead for the widow. (Is.1:16–17)*

In such a transformed society, people "will hammer their swords into plowshares, their spears into sickles. Nations will not lift sword against nation, there will be no more training for war." (Is. 2:4)

Isaiah's vision of a future society involved both an earthly hope and a spiritual ambition:

> *Once more there will be poured on us*
> *the spirit from above;*

*then shall the wilderness be fertile land*
*and fertile land become forest.*

*In the wilderness justice will come to live*
*and integrity in the fertile land;*
*integrity will bring peace,*
*justice give lasting security. (Is. 32:15–16)*

Transformation takes place at both levels: a wilderness becomes fertile and livable; virtues of justice and integrity change the patterns of human life.

But the challenges and dreams of Isaiah, Jeremiah, and the earlier phophets went unheeded in Israel. In 587 Jerusalem was conquered and the Israelites were led into exile, their dreams shattered. In the second part of the book of Isaiah, written during this time, a new and powerful dream is imagined: the vision of a servant of Yahweh, a savior who will heal and restore their life. Second Isaiah invites these exiles to dream again:

*Here is my servant who I uphold,*
*my chosen one in whom my soul delights.*
*I have endowed him with my spirit*
*that he may bring true justice to the nations. (Is. 41:1)*

The dream, begun in Abraham's ambition to find a new home and revived in the early Israelites' vision of a land flowing with milk and honey, was undergoing a powerful transformation. This collective hope could not be simply identified with a national state, nor could it exclude the poor and the distressed. In their experience of the Exile the Israelites were again forced to revise, to reenvision their collective dream. Would this future place of justice and love be more interior than external, a realm founded more on personal conviction than on territorial sovereignty?

In the centuries between the Exile and the time of Christ, a new and powerful mood began to sweep through the Middle East. There was a growing sense that the end of the world was near. This pervasive expectation of a sudden end to our world, which survived into the time of Christ and the New Testament, turned Jewish thoughts to another world. Perhaps the dream of a place of peace and justice was not to be realized in this world but belonged instead to an afterlife, a truly "heavenly" land. It was during this period that the phrase *the kingdom of God* made its first and only appearance in the Jewish scriptures. God, in her feminine form as Wisdom, assists the virtuous person: "She showed him the kingdom of God and taught him the knowledge of holy things" (Wis. 10:10). During these centuries Jewish debate continued about the locus of this dreamed-of society—whether it is in this world or in another world—and wielded a powerful influence on the first generation of Christians.

In the New Testament, Jesus sees his own life and that of his followers as committed to this kingdom of God. His own ministry begins in Mark's gospel with the announcement, "The kingdom of God is at hand" (Mk. 1:15). The urgency of personal change and conversion so central to Jesus' concerns in the New Testament arises from the imminence of this kingdom. This long-dreamed-of kingdom is, in fact, the substance of Jesus' *good news*. The good news to be proclaimed is that this society and way of life, with its healing and transformation, is about to happen. (See especially Lk. 9.)

If there is great ambiguity in the New Testament about the kingdom of God—is it to happen only with the end of the world, or is it already happening in our lives?[2]—we can see that Jesus' life and the gospels are centrally concerned with the realization of this collective dream. In many parables, whether of planting (Mk. 4) or of wedding feasts (Mt. 22), Jesus stresses the imminence of this new life. In his sermon on the mount, he celebrates the poor who inherit this kingdom. In an encounter with the followers of John the Baptist, when they enquire if Jesus is the messiah, the dreamed-of one, Jesus tells them to report to John what they have seen: "The blind see again, the lame walk, lepers are cleansed, and the deaf hear, the dead are raised to life, the Good News is proclaimed to the poor" (Lk. 7:22). These personal and social changes are signs

---

2. Numerous times Jesus suggests that the kingdom is entered at death; during his final supper with his friends, he announces that he will not eat or drink again "until the kingdom comes." (See Mk. 14 and Lk. 22). Yet when he is pressed at another time to clarify when and how the kingdom will appear, he surprises his questioners: "You must know that the kingdom of God is among you." (Lk. 17:21) As we will suggest later in this section, the ambiguity of the New Testament must be retained: the kingdom of God belongs to both the present and the future.

of the kingdom; this is how we can recognize the realization of the dream in our own lives.

Toward the close of Matthew's gospel we find a scenario of the last judgment. This is a time when the faithful will "inherit the kingdom prepared for you from the foundation of the world" (Mt. 25:34). What actions have merited this realization of the dream? "I was hungry and you gave me food; I was thirsty and you gave me drink; I was a stranger and you made me welcome; naked and you clothed me, sick and you visited me, in prison and you came to see me . . ." These actions of justice and love, of caring for "one of the least of the brethren" bring a person into the dreamed-of and hoped-for kingdom of God. In these gospel accounts of the kingdom, it is made clear that our own actions contribute to or frustrate the realization of God's dream.

The whole of the gospels may be seen as an account of Jesus joining his own life ambition to the dream of the kingdom of God. His own actions—compassionately healing some while accusing others of falseness and injustice; his intense involvement with others alternating with periods of retreat and quiet—are guided by a vision of a certain style of life. Concern for healing and personal change overshadowed any concern for a strict observance of the many laws of Jewish life. And life clearly had an urgency to it: God's kingdom is about to be realized and we must change our lives, now, to fit God's ambition.

Despite his understanding of and enthusiasm for this dream of the kingdom of God, Jesus was himself surprised and confused by its development. Though he came to Jerusalem sensing danger, it was only in the garden of olives that he saw how radically different were God's plans for him. Facing his own death, Jesus had to confront the frustration and failure of his life ambition and dream. His vision of many more years of healing and challenge, of strengthening his friends in this new way of life—this dream was being broken. His own dream for his life was being purified and revised by his Father. Quite naturally, he resisted. He struggled against his death and the end of his dream of how the kingdom was to be realized. Yet in the end he came to trust the movement of his Father's dream and he came to see that the dream he had been nourishing and following did not belong to him; his own life and ambition belonged, finally, to the larger dream of the kingdom of

God, a dream always being realized in strange and confusing ways. In Jesus' death, his earlier life ambition was lost. And in this loss and death, a new vision and dream began to live. The particular dream that would in time be called "Christian" began to grow. Its peculiarity is its conviction (reinforced in the personal experience of believers) that our dreams and careers and vocations are not our own and that they grow by dying. Christians understand their own life ambitions and visions as gifts, as more than their own possessions. Neither owning nor fully controlling our own lives and careers, we expect them to be changed—sometimes in surprising or even painful ways—as we mature. The cross stands at the center of Christian faith and Christian dreaming—not out of morbidity, but out of the realization that this is how we grow. Vocations and dreams rigidly adhered to become idols; ambitions too strongly defended, made invulnerable, are not Christian. Christian dreams, named for the person who most powerfully shapes our dreaming, are expected to change as they become purified and come to match the dream that God is dreaming for all of us.

If Jesus Christ reenvisioned the dream of the kingdom of God, subsequent generations of believers have given their own interpretations of this collective hope. At certain times the kingdom has come to be emphatically identified with another world beyond this "vale of tears." Pessimistic about changing this world, Christians have longed for the realization of their dreams in heaven. At other times the dream of the kingdom of God has been given a very earthly shape: this dream of justice and social transformation is happening or could be happening in our own lives here and now. Social and political life are meant to reflect and pursue Christian values that have the power to change *this* world. This orientation to the dream of the kingdom, rather than urging patience until the end, urges an energetic participation in changing society according to the vision of social life given us in the scriptures.

The ambiguity of this dream—is it realizable in any way in our present society, or does it lie totally beyond us; can we contribute to its realization or is its coming exclusively the work of God—this ambiguity reminds us that Christian responses to this dream will range along a continuum. At one extreme will be those Christians convinced that the kingdom of God has nothing to do with this world; we can only hope and pray for deliverance from this sinful world and inclusion in God's heavenly world to come. At the other extreme of the continuum stand those Christians convinced that the kingdom of God is to be realized in this world through some specific political party or program. If the former extreme neglects the connections between social responsibility and heaven's rewards, the latter extreme too easily identifies its own dreams and agenda with God's. Between these extremes range the various and pluriform efforts of Christian communities to be faithful to this powerful dream which is at once within our responsibility and beyond our grasp.

The specific way that the vision of the kingdom is dreamed and pursued will be determined by the shape and vitality of each Christian community. As the dream of the kingdom of God is concretized in a faith community, it is mediated and made available to individual Christians.

### Christian Community: Mediator of the Dream

The dream of the kingdom of God does not exist in the abstract nor only in the written pages of the New Testament. It survives and thrives in individual communities of faith. This inherited hope is dreamed again in the lives of believing Christians. The kingdom of God is rescued from being only a utopian vision as it attains recognizable shape in the lives of Christians in particular communities of faith.

But a Christian community is not merely a collection of individual dreams and hopes. Each faith community, as it matures, develops its own sense of purpose, its own Christian hope and vision. A Christian community—parish, diocese, school, hospital, congregation—is a meeting ground of individual vocations and the collective dream of the kingdom of God. The maturing of a community can be charted by its efforts to interpret the dream of the kingdom concretely in the light of its own insights and needs. This effort of a community to define its own sense of purpose is, in fact, a growing into its own vocation. The clarification of a faith community's dream and ambition gives the inherited dream of the kingdom concrete and visible expression. It is also the way a community performs one of its central functions—mediating to its members the dream of the kingdom of God.

This ministry of mediating the Christian dream of the kingdom begins in the community's awareness of its own dream and vocation. Hopefully, this will be a shared, lively, and practical dream. A community's ambition or mission must be a shared one; if it is a plan imported or announced "from on high" it will be less effective in moving these Christians to action. It must also be a lively dream—one that excites us, one that is more than a distant memory of "what we have always done" or a vague guilt about "what we ought to do." It must also be a somewhat practical vision—a hope that is pursuable, that finds expression in the community's specific and daily decisions about such things as education, finances, and liturgy.

The dream or vocation of a faith community shares an important characteristic of an individual vocation: it is a *partial* expression of the dream of the kingdom. A community must not confuse its own hope and ambition with the kingdom itself. The kingdom of God is God's dream for us; a community's dream is this group's response (always partial and incomplete) to that gift of hope. A community's dream, like an individual vocation, stands in constant need of purification.

The liveliness of a faith community arises from its shared vision and clarity of purpose. A vital community is one that is excited by the dream of the kingdom, the vision of a society transformed by justice and love. Its energies are aroused by and directed toward the realization of this dream.

But a community's dream shares the vicissitudes and fragility of individual vocations. A group's vision grows and matures, but it can also wither and become lost. A community may lose its dream, just as individual believers may allow their own religious hopes to die. When this happens to a community, liturgies and Sunday collections may continue, but the vision is gone. Members are rhetorically exhorted to follow the gospel, but there is no longer any excitement or ambition to change the world in a Christian direction.

As a faith community loses its vision, it begins to forfeit its function as mediator of dreams. Vocations of individual believers— whether vocations to a committed Christian life as married or single Christians, or to the priesthood or religious life—begin to wither. In the absence of a strong corporate dream in the community (with attractive examples of its being lived out), individuals turn to other life ambitions. The Christian values of love and justice penetrate less powerfully the lives of individual believers as the dream of the kingdom of God becomes more remote and less believable.

If a community can lose its dream, it can also allow it to narrow into a rigid and compulsive vision. Often this happens when a community seizes one aspect of Christian life (for example, being born again or the right to life or political activism) and gives it exclusive and obsessive attention. Being born again in this community becomes a credential of holiness, of being holier than others. In its enthusiasm for an unborn child's right to life, a community may neglect other concerns of Christian justice and mercy. Our sense that we must "take a stand" politically can close us to the questions or challenges or alternative insights of other Christians. Such simplifying of the complex vision of the kingdom leads easily to a kind of idolatry: this partial vision is identified with the realization of the kingdom itself. A single action or conviction establishes one's orthodoxy and goodness. Antagonistic defense of "our vision" replaces a broader and more open pursuit of the elusive kingdom. A community's dream, like that of an individual, can become a tyranny. Like any tyranny or compulsion, such a dream is recognized by its rigidity and lack of freedom. Defending its narrowed vision of "what we must do to be saved," it tends to neglect its need for continuing purification.

**Mediating the Dream**

This mediation begins, as we have observed, with a community's clarification of its own dream. As it gives the vision of the kingdom of God more immediate and tangible force, a community "traditions" this collective dream of Christian faith. How specifically does this mediation occur and what perils may be expected along the way?

In every liturgical celebration and educational effort, a faith community announces its dream. It may be a withered dream, or a compulsive vision, or an exciting hope, but in its public actions a community hands on some version of the Christian dream. The religious education or, perhaps better, the religious formation of the members of the community depends on this dream. *Religious formation* has in Roman Catholic parlance usually referred to the initial education of priests and vowed religious. Yet religious formation is what any faith community is about; the vitality of the community's dream is crucial to this religious formation of all its members.

In the religious formation of a new member of a faith community, the community invites the individual to join her dream to the corporate vision of the group. The assumption here is that both the community and the individual have a dream. The balance between the individual and the corporate dream is most important. A faith community is not a neutral zone in which individuals pursue their vocations. Nor does a community provide vocations for individuals who would otherwise be directionless. Recognizing that God is at work in all believers (exciting them to life ambitions which contribute to the kingdom of God), a community of faith invites its members to pursue their vocations as part of the community's larger dream and purpose. Further, a community exemplifies for individuals many specific ways of pursuing the dream of the kingdom. It displays—in its liturgies and programs for social justice, in the lives of its talented and concerned members—the Christian dream at work. The individual is invited to let his dream and vocation grow into and contribute to this community's dream.

The ministry of a faith community to its young adults begins in exciting them with the dream of the kingdom. It tells the young that such a dream exists; it tells them that—in part, because of this community—it is a believable dream. This ministry continues as the young are helped to clarify their own dreams and Christian ambitions. Without such a vital community context, a Christian might understandably find the kingdom of God unbelievable. But the delicate balance between individual and community vocation can be easily disturbed. When individuals are confused or frightened by their own dreams, they may substitute a community's dream for their own. A community—a religious order, parish, or school—may present such a clear and stable vision of Christian life that I too quickly slip into the community dream rather than attending to my own slowly growing vocation. The failure here (becoming the doctor my parents want me to be, or the priest that my pastor had hoped I would be) is not one of wrongdoing but of following a dream that is not genuinely mine. Often it is only after several decades of pursuing someone else's vocation or dream that such a person feels the call to return to a dream deferred or a vocation ignored.

If a community's corporate dream mediates the vision of the kingdom to individuals, it is also challenged and changed by individual dreams. Every human dream of the kingdom—and this includes every individual and every community in the Church—remains in need of purification. Sometimes this purifying of a community's dream happens as some individuals in the group dream new dreams. Some members of a parish dream of the community spending more of its energy and other resources for social justice concerns; several members of a Catholic hospital begin to envision a more effective way of caring for the very poor; some women today are dreaming dreams of priestly ministry. Such dreams are often threatening because they challenge the adequacy and stability of the group's dream. Disturbing as they are to our accustomed ways of dreaming and experiencing our faith, we may judge these new dreams to be mere illusions, or to be enthusiasms that will soon disappear. Yet we know that such new dreams lead, at times, to a purifying of the dream of this community and even that of the larger Church. New dreams can break open collective hopes that have become too rigid; they can challenge ambitions that have grown too safe and shortsighted. Our own religious heritage has been profoundly affected by individual dreams breaking into and altering our collective dream. Think of the ambitions and hopes of Francis of Assisi, Catherine of Siena, Ignatius Loyola. But this same dynamic also happens in more ordinary ways in our faith communities today. If it is confusing, it is also to be expected. The collective dream of this community supports and challenges the growth of individual vocations, just as these individual dreams contribute to and, at times, challenge the community's dream. And both dreams, individual and corporate, must remain open to the enlivening criticism and purification provided by God's dream of the kingdom.

When we reflect on the dynamic relationship between individual vocations and community dreams, it is useful to recall another mediator of dreams: the family. As we have discussed in our book *Marrying Well*, the family is a most active arena of dreams. Parents are busy not only with the growth of their own life ambitions but with the fostering of their childrens' dreams. An inner discipline of Christian family life is learning to distinguish our own dreams from those fragile, beginning dreams of our children. Neither neglecting our children's dreams nor forcing them into the mold of our frustrated hopes, as parents we learn slowly and painfully the lesson of Christian stewardship: we are the guardians and nurturers of dreams and vocations that we neither control nor fully understand.

But a family is not only a collection of individual dreams. A family understandably develops its own collective dream: this group of people—responding to the many invitations of God that have both brought them together and put them in tension with each other—gradually forges its own set of values and hopes. The life style and decisions that give this family its uniqueness also define its dream of Christian life. Such a family dream is, of course, extraordinarily fragile. The busyness of everyday life and fatigue distracts us from one another; we often seem to lack the time to share our deepest hopes. And so our common Christian hopes can be lost, or at least rarely celebrated. Also, a family dream can be warped until it becomes the dream of only one parent to which the other family members are constrained. But when this fragile dream of a family matures, it fulfills the rhetoric of our faith: the family becomes a domestic Church. In practical, everyday life, the dream of the kingdom of God becomes believable among us.

Finally, a faith community's mediating of the dream will have moments of special urgency. The period of late adolescence and early adulthood, when individual life ambitions and dreams are being tested, is one of these times. How can a community best respond to this *kairos* or special time for these young people? What programs of support and challenge and clarification might communities provide for them as they wrestle with powerful and confusing ambitions? Whatever the response, this ministry must be rooted in the community's clarity about its own maturing dream and sense of purpose.

A second time for a community's special ministry to the dream is midlife. Community members in their forties and fifties, as we have suggested, can be expected to hear inner invitations toward reconciliations with their life ambitions. Although these reconciliations may take very different shapes, they will always be an opportunities for special grace. How might a community better minister to its adults at these times? How can we better alert adult Christians to the expectable challenges of God in midlife so they will be neither ashamed of movements of dissatisfaction and reevaluation, nor left to undergo these purifications alone?

As "God moves in mysterious ways," so do the journeys of our lives. Young adulthood and midlife are not the only places where our dream or career or life ambition may demand special attention. Every crisis in our significant relationships and in our work can threaten or break a life dream. Losing a job, the death of a child, divorce, retirement—at different times, often unanticipated, the direction of our life is altered and our plans come under serious review. Many of these times have found little ministerial response from the Christian community in the past. Today, better aware that God is at work (or is it "at play"?) in every movement of our life, we are beginning to devise ministries that respond more carefully and effectively to these crises when a dream is broken or demands a radical reconciliation. The Christian community, as mediator of the dream, is learning to minister more gracefully to its members as their own vocations and dreams die and rise and are purified by the dream of the kingdom of God.

**Imagination and Prophecy**

Our Christian lives mature in the interplay of three dreams: our own vocations are excited and shaped by our inherited vision of the kingdom of God; a faith community mediates this collective dream to us by giving it concrete expression in this time and place. The survival and growth of these Christian dreams are central tasks of ministry. Our reflection here will conclude with three questions. Is the dream of the kingdom of God real or imaginary? How does a community's own dream survive? Where does the dream abide?

Our vision of the kingdom of God is itself a gift of faith. We sense that, alone, we could not generate such an improbable, yet compelling image of the future. And even when we are gifted with this appealing image of the future, we are always close to losing it. The evidence against such a possibility is staggering: the blind will see? the poor will be cared for? Unbelievers scoff at such an illusion. How are we, as believers, to deal with this ambiguous and persistent hope that identifies us as Christians?

Our response is to seize this dream's full ambiguity. This hope is always being realized and always being frustrated. The improbable dream of the kingdom is being realized and fulfilled in every act of care and reconciliation and justice we undertake. Every action, personal and corporate, noticed and unnoticed, of Christian care and healing brings about the kingdom. The kingdom of God is always coming, constantly happening—in us and despite us. Each of these "comings" calls for celebration because our hope is at once so fragile and so unrelenting. Further, this experience of the kingdom's practical realization teaches us our active role in it: it is within our power; we participate in the coming of the kingdom of God. But, as we well know, this is but half the story.

If the kingdom is always being realized, it is also and simultaneously being frustrated. Every personal and communal act of rejecting "others" as unlike us, and every act of destructive anger or selfishness frustrates this dream. These acts, in us and in others, argue that the dream is nonsense and a mere fantasy. Every act of the institutional Church that is self-centered or defensive works against this dream. The dream of the kingdom is always being frustrated—not just by "demonic" systems of government or the impersonal greed of multinational corporations, but by believers and by the Church itself. If this is a source of scandal among us, it also helps to remind us that the Church is *not* the kingdom but its (often faithful) servant. All our Christian efforts of justice and love are directed ultimately not to the justification or aggrandizing of the Church, but to the coming of the kingdom of God.

In moments of reflection we can all recognize ways in which we frustrate the realization of this collective dream. This recognition serves to balance our sense of efficacy in the coming of the kingdom. If the realization of this dream is in part our responsibility, it also lies beyond us. It is a dream that originates in God; it is a way of life that God is dreaming into reality. As surely as we participate in the bringing of the kingdom, we also recognize that it is beyond us. It is at once within our responsibility and beyond our grasp. This ambiguity need not cripple our efforts or reduce us to passivity. It can, instead, sober us. This modesty protects us from identifying the kingdom with a single social program or political strategy. It protects us from confusing the Church with the kingdom. And it can give us the perspective that will see us through the many failures and frustrations necessarily involved in pursuing over a lifetime so ambitious a hope for humankind.

The second question asks: how does a community's dream survive and flourish? This survival of the dream within the local community of believers depends on a very special ministry. A traditional name for this has been the ministry of prophecy. A more contemporary term might be the ministry of the imagination. Dreams are products of the imagination. If we can believe that it is (often) God who ignites and guides our imaginations, then its images may be more than flimsy fantasies. A prophet is someone who en-visions, who can see into and see through what is going on in human life. Imagination is the faculty, the organ of prophecy. All ministries depend on a vision—a glimpse of where we are going, of what we are struggling for. Imaginative people in our midst provide that vision: they see, or more exactly, renew the vision that God has been providing us. They see again, in exciting images and evocative detail, a future transformed by Christian love and justice. Remembering the ancient dream, they rekindle it in new and powerful images. They awaken us to it and make us hopeful again. Prophecy and the ministry of the imagination wither when we come to think that all the dreams have already been dreamed. Then religious faith, begun in visions and images, becomes encased in dogma alone and the religious imagination is stilled.

Another way that the dream loses its liveliness is through distraction and fatigue. A community's ministers can easily become bogged down in maintaining the present institution with its many important programs. An absorbing maintenance of *now* eventually distracts us from the future and the coming of the kingdom. Our religious imaginations stand ready to pull us out of the present in pursuit of an unfinished future. Taking the time to imagine—even "wasting" the time in playful dreaming and fantasizing—we open ourselves to the changes, losses, and conversions that God's future will demand. The education of Christian ministers has for a long time trained us to deal better with the past and the present than with change and the future. We are, as a result, a rather serious and responsible lot, but often unimaginative. Neglect of the imagination imperils the survival and flourishing of Christian dreams.

A community's dream depends in part, then, on its dreamers. A community needs to welcome and support in its midst both those who help it act responsibly in regard to the compelling needs of the present and those who turn it toward the future. These prophets, these ministers of the imagination, help us to see the inadequacy of the present and to envision a radically different future. This vision, often expressed in stories and exciting images, revives the dream of the kingdom of God. It brings the kingdom of God into this community even as it points this community beyond itself and toward the kingdom.

The third question arises from the volatile and fragile nature of our Christian dreams. Where does the dream abide? One response to this question returns to the enigmatic statement of Luke: "The kingdom of God is within you" (Lk. 17:21). This sentence has traditionally been understood to refer to the "already" aspect of the kingdom. The presence of God is not some future fantasy; Jesus Christ has brought this future hope into human life. But we can still ask: where is it? how is it "within us"? This dream has become present for us because of Jesus Christ, and it is present in our imagination. The kingdom has arrived when it is powerfully alive in us, in our own dreams and imaginations. But it is yet to be fully and practically realized because it is still *mostly* in our hopes.

We have yet to dream this vision into reality. The dream of the kingdom of God is not simply beyond us, belonging only to God; if it were, we could not even imagine it. It is happening already, within us. Nor is this a private event, meant for our individual consolation. The "you" of the Greek New Testament is plural: "The kingdom of God is among you." This dream is alive in a group's hopes and ambitions.

This is good news for communities of faith. It means that the dream of the kingdom of God, dreamed relentlessly for three thousand years and more, is coming alive in *this* group. And as this group—this community—dares to dream, takes the time to listen to and clarify its own hopes and Christian ambitions, it provides the fertile, prophetic context in which individual vocations and dreams will grow.


## FOR FURTHER REFLECTION

To make this reflection on Christian dreams more concrete, it may be useful to consider the dream in your own life. In a mood of reflection and relaxation, recall your best and deepest hope for your own life. What is this dream in your life right now? Take time to let the images and hopes and feelings emerge.

Reflect, then, on how your dream has grown or changed over the past years. How does your present life ambition connect with your earlier hopes and goals? Have elements of an earlier dream been lost or let go? What new elements are part of your life dream now?

Then consider the community context of your own hopes. Does the most important community in your life—whether family or parish or religious congregation—have a dream that is strong and active? Is this community itself in a process of clarifying or changing its dream? How do your hopes fit these communal dreams and ambitions—how do they confirm each other? are there ways in which they conflict?

Finally, it may be fruitful to situate your hopes in the context of the dream of the kingdom of God. How do you see your life goals related to Christ's vision of a more just and caring society? How does your community's dream contribute to the coming of the kingdom? How is it challenged by the dream of the kingdom of God?

## ADDITIONAL RESOURCES

Daniel Levinson has studied the role of the dream as a developing life ambition in *The Seasons of a Man's Life* (New York: Alfred A. Knopf, 1978). We have examined this aspect of human development in light of Christian spirituality and religious maturing: see Chapter 5, "Religious Generativity," in our *Christian Life Patterns* (New York: Doubleday & Co., 1979) and Chapter 12, "Identity: Vocation and Marriage," in our *Marrying Well: Possibilities in Christian Marriage Today* (New York: Doubleday & Co., 1981).

Rudolf Schnackenburg's important discussion of the image of the kingdom of God is found in his *God's Rule and Kingdom* (New York: Herder & Herder, 1963). For another excellent exploration of Jesus' use of this image, see Norman Perrin's *Jesus and the Language of the Kingdom* (Philadelphia: Fortress Press, 1976). Jon Sobrino, in his *Christology at the Crossroads* (New York: Orbis Books, 1978), examines the kingdom of God from the perspective of liberation theology: see, especially, his discussion of the relation of social sin to the coming of the kingdom in Chapter 3. For a discussion of the role of the "basic community church" in the ministry of transforming the world, see Johann Baptist Metz, *The Emergent Church* (New York: Crossroad Publishing Co., 1981).

# ❖ PART IV

---

# PARTICIPATING
# IN COMMUNITY

# 8 ✢
# PERSONAL STRENGTHS FOR COMMUNITY

Community, as an arena of dreams and as a special form of group life, provides both challenges and opportunities. In the following four chapters we wish to explore the psychological aspects of community—the interpersonal dynamics at work in this kind of group life and the personal resources necessary for its successful pursuit. Our discussion will begin in a consideration of intimacy and mutuality.

To participate effectively in a community, I must be able both to experience its support and to meet its demands. This requires resources of both mind and heart. These strengths for personal involvement in group life are described by psychologists as resources of intimacy. As the word is used here, intimacy is more than a synonym for sexual experience or romantic love. Intimacy refers to the resources I have for being close to other people. It is these strengths of intimacy that enable me to tolerate both the exhilaration and the strain that are inevitably a part of continuing close relationships. My resources for intimacy come into play across a range of relationships—friendship, work collaboration, community living. Whenever there is personal disclosure and mutuality, the resources of intimacy are involved. A well-developed ability to be intimate enables me to be with different persons in a rich variety of ways, ways that are appropriate to my own personality and life style and to the demands of different situations. It is upon these resources of intimacy that I draw in my attempts to live closely with others, to offer my talents to a common vision, to share my life and hopes with other people.

To help situate intimacy in a broadened context, one that goes beyond sexuality and romance, let us consider a crisis of intimacy that may arise in the course of my work. I volunteer as a member of a work group where coordination and cooperation are necessary for the successful completion of our task. This may be a group at work, at school, in my church, or in the neighborhood. As our work goes on I begin to feel uncomfortable. It is not that any one person is dominating the group or impeding its work. But my suggestion is only one among many. My work is affected by what the others do. My contributions look different to me after the group has dealt with them. I feel that things are not going as they should, as I expected they would. There is an impulse to gain greater control of the situation ("if only I could get them to do it my way!"), countered by an impulse to withdraw ("clearly, these people don't appreciate what I have to offer; it would probably be better for me to go off on my own"). I vacillate in an experience of increasing discomfort and disorientation. But what is being threatened here? What is in danger of being lost? It is my very self. I am afraid others may overwhelm me, absorbing my identity as well as my ideas.

There are parallels here with the ambiguous experience of drawing close to another person in friendship and love. There are obvious differences, but the dynamic is the same. There is the threat of some loss of self. The temptation to flee is mixed with a desire to control the situation. Both these impulses are accompanied by an inclination to stay with the uneasiness, in the hope of finding a better way of being together and working together.

These examples put us in touch with an underlying dynamic in community. There is a normal, expectable tension that most of us experience when we come "up close," whether in work or in friendship. The tension is generated by a very basic concern—if I come close to you, will I survive? Will my idea survive, if I share it with this group? Will my plan survive, if I bring it up in this committee? Will I survive— my sense of who I am, my self-esteem, my hopes for what I can become—if I let these other people close enough to influence me?

These are the questions, then, at the threshold of intimacy: Am I sure enough of myself that I can risk being close to other people? Am I comfortable enough with my sense of "who I am" that I can afford to let you close enough to see for yourself? Am I confident enough of my own ability that I can take the chance of being influenced by yours? I can expect to have to face these questions myself, at one time or another, as a part of my efforts to participate in community.

Every community asks its members to share some significant part of their lives. The sharing that is appropriate in this particular community—among the religious education faculty of a diocesan high school, for example—may not bring us together in deep personal friendship, but it will require openness and self-disclosure. I am asked here to share with these other faculty members some important part of myself—my values, ideals, talents, ideas. This disclosure leaves me vulnerable: some part of my sense of myself is open to confirmation or to challenge or, perhaps, to change.

Community involves an overlapping of space, a willingness to be influenced, an openness to the possibility of change. To participate in community I must be able to come close to others in ways that enable them to know, to influence, and possibly to alter my sense of who I am. I must accept the risk of being changed, of coming to a different awareness of myself, as a result of this encounter. If I am unsure of who I am, then this risk may seem too great. Close contact with other people may seem a threat since they can force upon me new information that challenges my fragile sense of self. To protect myself, I may develop a rigid interpersonal style that keeps others at a distance and leaves little room for mutuality.

## Community and Friendship

For many of us, community is especially attractive in its promise of honest communication and mutual support. We sense that relationships in community hold the possibility of "more"; here at least we will be able to move beyond the barriers that so often separate us from one another. Often it is a desire for this "more" that draws us to a community group. Here we hope to be able to experience a richer kind of relationship than we know in much of the rest of our lives. And, as we have seen, this hope is not simply an illusion. As intermediate styles of group life, communities are likely to encourage members to share each other's lives and values to a greater degree than do most of the formal organizations and task-oriented groups to which adults belong. But sometimes the "more" of community is translated in the image of close friendship, and here confusion can begin. Experiences of close friendship and love are crucial to personal development—on this point both personal experience and the findings of psychological research concur. In a particular case it may happen that our experience together in a community group develops into this special bond of deep mutuality. But it is risky for close friendship to become the goal of a community's life or the criterion of its success. This is not because friendship is suspect (either "dangerous" or "distracting" or "just for sissies"), but because *close friendship* and *community* are two kinds of relationships.

But to acknowledge that friendship and community are not the same is not to suggest that intimacy has no place in a community's life. Intimacy, in the sense that we are using the term in this chapter, is a key resource for community. My capacity for intimacy—for being "up close"—will be tested and strengthened in the many relationships that make up my participation in *this* community. We expect, and appropriately so, that interaction among us in community will be more meaningful than the more limited and role-specified relationships that we know elsewhere. This is because community interaction involves greater openness, a sense of availability to one another, a real engagement in which mutuality plays an indispensable part. The dynamic of mutuality is important in community, involving all of us in a process of disclosing something of ourselves and responding to the information we receive from others. This disclosure and engagement may take place at many different levels—it may be our work that we share, or our religious values, or our common commitment to social reform. In a group that is a community both our ideas and our emotions will come into play, both what we can do and who we are. These are all experiences of intimacy, though for most of us they are of a somewhat different quality than is the particular—and even privileged—mutuality of close friendship. Later in this book Michael Cowan considers in greater detail the different levels of mutuality that can characterize community relationships.

## Cooperation and Competition

We have mentioned before that the term *intimacy* is most often used in regard to experiences of friendship and love. This usage is well founded, since for most of us it is in the experience of close friendship and mutual love that we have learned what is most important to us about being "up close." But, as we noted at the beginning of the chapter, adult intimacy takes us beyond the few special relationships of deep friendship into the broader range of experiences that bring us up close to others. For most adults, social experiences of cooperation and competition are important instances of intimacy. Whether in work or play, cooperation and competition test my self-awareness, my self-assurance, my empathy with others and my capacity for mutual interaction. Cooperation involves us in some joint action to accomplish a common goal. Competition puts us in opposition to one another in our pursuit of a goal that is important to us both. Both competition and cooperation are to be expected among us in community groups; both are normal dynamics in ongoing close relationships.

Some examples may help us see the connections of cooperation and competition with intimacy. Resources of intimacy are needed, for instance, in a meeting of the parish committee charged with planning the annual fund-raising spaghetti supper. The success of this event is crucial to the parish budget; without the proceeds of the supper we would have to double the tuition in the parish school and cut back our contribution to our sister parish in the inner city. To be a good cooperator in this committee I must, first, be aware of the particular contribution that I can make to our common goal—and this requires that I be aware of both my strengths and my limitations. I must be secure enough with these strengths that I can offer them to the group task, even with the risk that my offer may not always be accepted. I must be flexible enough to accept the modification of my own contribution by other people. I must have empathy enough to be able to take pride in what we have accomplished together, just as in other situations I rejoice in what I can accomplish on my own.

Without these resources, it will be difficult for me to cooperate well. For example, generosity may move me to offer to coordinate the plans for moving people in and out of the dining area. This job is central to the financial success of the fund-raiser: a bottleneck in the dining room means long lines, disgruntled parishioners, fewer meals served. But, as most of my friends and coworkers are aware, I am myself a very disorganized person. I am warm and gregarious and fun to be with, but I have a hard time making plans in advance or anticipating problems before they arise. I might be able to make a great contribution to the success of the supper by serving on a welcoming committee or by acting as master of ceremonies for the social that follows, but I am an unlikely candidate for dining-room coordinator. My offer to supervise the dining room may express my goodwill, but it does not really indicate that I am able to cooperate well. I lack, in this instance at least, the self-awareness that is necessary for effective cooperation. I am not clear about the particular contribution that I have to make to our common goal.

Self-awareness is essential for cooperation, as is some degree of self-confidence. I must be able to offer my help, to put forth my idea, to sketch out my plan—not always needing to be coaxed. For many of us it is not hard to recall a group situation where we were not confident enough to be very cooperative. I hold back my idea, afraid that it will strike others as farfetched or foolish. I am reluctant to volunteer my help ("suppose they really don't want me on their committee!") and wait instead to be asked. This reluctance is, obviously, not always inappropriate—but it often makes cooperation more difficult.

To be able to cooperate well also requires personal flexibility. Working together will mean that my ideas and plans are brought up close to yours. We can each expect this contact to have some effect on us. We may find we are in agreement from the start; our contact simply confirms and reinforces what we had before. But our interaction may have a different result—my idea may be questioned, your plan may be modified, we may each come to see things differently than we did before. In this process, I may begin to feel challenged, growing uncomfortable with the prospect that I may have to change. Or I may experience the process more as an opportunity for clarification and growth. This kind of personal flexibility—such an important resource in cooperation—is rooted in an awareness that change can be an expression of integrity as well as of compromise.

The advantages—to myself and to others—of my developing these psychological strengths of intimacy make cooperation a valued interpersonal ability. Competition, on the other hand, has a bad reputation. Many therapists, educators, and religious persons share the conviction that competition should be eliminated, at least as much as possible. This conviction is born of much experience with the negative effects of competition in the lives of individuals and in groups and organizations.

The negative effects of competition are, then, apparent to most of us. But many of us have also sensed that competition is not simply negative. While not denying the problematic aspects of competition, we would like to consider another side of this admittedly ambiguous phenomenon. Most psychologists today would attest that an ability to compete maturely is an important ingredient of the adult personality. And the psychological characteristics of the mature competitor are remarkably similar to those of the mature cooperator. To compete well—in sports, for example—I must have a realistic sense of my own abilities, with an awareness of both the strong and weak points in my game. But here, too, self-knowledge is not enough. I must know my game, but then I must also play it. Competition forces me to express my abilities, to expose them to the test of a concrete challenge, with the risk that they may not be sufficient. (If I only play the games that I am sure ahead of time I will win, I am not likely to be considered a good competitor.) To compete is to take a chance, to be able to take a risk. When I compete I play my game—not in order to fail—but with the realization that in any one instance my current level of strength or skill may not be sufficient to prevail. But it is only in taking that risk of failure that I can confirm and develop my strengths. Finally, the exchange of competition reveals much about each participant. In the contest I come to a better knowledge of myself and to a special awareness of my opponent. My success in the game is often dependent upon flexibility and creativity in modifying myself in response to what I learn about my rival.

These characteristics—awareness of myself and the other person, a sense of self adequate to the demand of mutuality and to the possibility of failure, flexible response to the individuality of other persons—are not of value in sports alone. They are resources that enhance the adult personality. These abilities are valuable in a variety of community relationships—team work, conflict resolution, negotiation, planning. They are intimacy resources often lacking in persons who cannot—or do not—compete.

The mature personality has available a range of psychological resources and a repertoire of varied behaviors. The competent adult is capable of both cooperation and competition and can discern when, and in what combination, each is appropriate.

## Psychological Resources of Community

These, then, are some of the social contexts of intimacy in community life. In my struggle to find a personally appropriate response to the demands of each, I come into more confident possession of my own resources for intimacy. It is upon these resources that I draw as I participate in the various group settings that are a part of my own experience.

The psychological resources that help me to participate well in community groups include:

- A flexible sense of myself, which includes a basic awareness and acceptance of who I am, along with some openness to new information;
- An awareness of other people that includes empathy or the capacity to see things from their point of view;
- A willingness to be influenced by this awareness, to modify myself in response to new information and to the requirements of different interpersonal situations.

Mature intimacy involves the flexibility to incorporate these changes into my personality in a way that strengthens rather than diminishes me. It helps me to be creative in devising with other people patterns of behavior and life style that are mutually enhancing. And finally, my resources for intimacy include some tolerance for the inevitable strain involved in personal accommodation and compromise.

In *Identity: Youth and Crisis,* psychologist Erik Erikson describes intimacy (as a psychological strength and resource of the personality) as "the capacity to commit oneself to concrete affiliations and partnerships and to develop the ethical strength to abide by such commitments, even though they may call for significant sacrifice and compromise." Intimacy is, then, a capacity, an ability, an abiding competence of adult maturity. It is the strength that enables me to commit myself, not to humankind in general or to idealized movements, but to particular persons in concrete relationships—aware of the limitation and incompleteness that are involved. Intimacy resources are drawn upon again in the living out of these commitments. Relationships are not static; people change and relationships develop over time. Some developments will bring fulfillment; others will make demands for accommodation, for understanding, for tolerance, for forgiveness. A well-developed capacity for intimacy enables me to sustain the adjustments and compromises of life with others, without jeopardy to my own integrity. A flexible identity, an empathic awareness of others, an openness to continued development of the self—these strengths make creative commitment possible. They are invaluable resources for participation in community.

The person who has responded successfully to the challenges of intimacy is not one who experiences no fear of the loss of self in close contact with others, but one who has confronted this fear. Maturity does not eliminate the impulse toward isolation; it puts it in the service of the self. Intimacy and isolation may be seen as poles of a continuum along which my relationships fall. The ability to set myself off from others, to be selective in my love, to seek and savor periods of solitude—these are as important indicators of my capacity for adult intimacy as are cooperation or mutual support.

## FOR FURTHER REFLECTION

Consider your own experience of the resources of intimacy. Begin by bringing back to your memory the many relationships that are an important part of your own life now—relationships with friends and loved ones, with coworkers, in communal living, in committee work. Then select a recent instance in which you were with one or several of these persons in a significant way. The experience may be positive or negative; it may involve a situation in your work, at home, in friendship, in the parish. Spend some time recalling the details of this particular experience—the events, the persons, the feelings, the outcome—and why it is significant for you. Then turn to these questions.

1. What does this particular experience say to you about your own strengths for intimacy, about the resources you bring to being up close to other people?

2. What does it say to you about your own frustrations in being close to other people, about your limitations in regard to intimacy?

3. Have you encountered any new ideas here concerning ways in which you want to improve your ways of being with other people, ways in which your own resources for intimacy may be strengthened?

## ADDITIONAL RESOURCES

Erik Erikson discusses his now-classic understanding of intimacy as a psychological resource in Chapter 7 of *Childhood and Society*, second edition (New York: W.W. Norton & Co., 1963) and in Chapter 3 of *Identity: Youth and Crisis* (New York: W.W. Norton & Co., 1968). An expanded consideration of intimacy as a psychological resource and as a religious virtue may be found in Chapter 4, "Intimacy and Religious Growth," in our *Christian Life Patterns* (New York: Doubleday & Co., 1979) and in Chapter 13, "Intimacy—The Virtue at the Heart of Marriage," in our *Marrying Well* (New York: Doubleday & Co., 1981).

In *The Psychological Sense of Community* (San Francisco: Jossey-Bass, 1974) Seymour Sarason describes community as a psychological reality and calls attention to the contribution of this reality to the success of social service and other helping efforts. Dorothy Lee discusses the positive and negative effects of community upon individuality in *Valuing the Self* (Englewood Cliffs, NJ: Prentice-Hall, 1976).

Two important religious discussions of intimacy as a psychological reality are found in *The Family in Crisis or in Transition* (New York: The Seabury Press, 1979), edited by Andrew Greeley. These are John Shea's "A Theological Perspective on Human Relations Skills and Family Intimacy," and "The Catholic Model of Caritas: Self-transcendence and Transformation" by David Tracy. Henri Nouwen considers the role that intimacy, ministry, prayer, and solitude play in community in *Clowning in Rome* (New York: Doubleday & Co., 1979).

# 9 ✤
# Communication and Conflict in Community

Community brings us up close—that is in large part its power and its attraction. But being up close, whether in friendship or community living or collaborative work, is not always easy. In order to realize the possibilities of community, we need, as we saw in Chapter 8, resources of psychological maturity: a sense of who I am, an openness to others, a capacity for commitment, some tolerance for the ambiguity both in myself and in other people. But these resources may not be enough. Aptitudes for intimacy must be expressed in behavior. We must be able, in the give and take of our interaction, to develop ways of being together and working together that are mutually satisfying. Our desire to be close to other people must be expressed in the way we act toward one another. It is encouraging to know that we can get better at being up close. We can learn more satisfying ways to act, more appropriate ways to give and receive the gift of ourselves that is at the core of effective communication. And among the most valuable resources for this growth are the skills of community living.

## The Skills of Community

Over the past two decades there has been much interest within psychology and other disciplines in better understanding what happens in communication between people. As a result, we are more clearly aware today of both what helps and what frustrates understanding in close relationships. Values and attitudes are important to our ability to live and work closely with others, but so, especially, is our behavior. There are skillful—that is, effective—

ways to be with and behave toward one another. Interpersonal skills that are especially important for community living include empathy, personal disclosure, and confrontation. Each involves both attitudes and behaviors; each can contribute significantly to our interaction within community settings.

Empathy enables me to understand another person from within that person's frame of reference. Empathy begins in an attitude of openness which enables me to set aside my own concerns and turn myself toward you. But this basic openness may not be enough. My capacity for empathy can be enhanced by my developing a range of behavioral skills. An accepting posture, attentive listening, sensitive paraphrasing—each of these can contribute to my effective presence to you.

My posture can give you important information about who you are to me and how important I judge your communication to be. If I appear distracted or edgy, if I keep glancing at my watch or rush to take an incoming phone call, I am likely to make you feel that you are not very important to me now. If, on the other hand, I turn my chair toward you when you sit down, if I make eye contact and seem relaxed, you are more likely to sense that I am really here for you.

Learning to listen well is another important skill of community interaction. To listen is to pay attention: paying attention is a receptive, but not a passive, attitude. If I cannot pay attention it will be difficult for me to hear; if I do not listen it will be difficult for me to understand and to respond effectively to you. To listen well is to listen actively, alert to the full context of the message. The skills of active listening are those behaviors which enable me to be aware of your full message. This includes my being alert to your words and their nuance. But equally and often even more important are the nonverbal factors involved. Your tone of voice, your gestures, the timing, the emotional content—these may tell me more than the words between us. To listen actively, then, calls for an awareness of the content, the feelings, and the context of our communication.

Sensitive paraphrasing is a skill of empathy as well. I show you that I understand you by repeating back to you the essence of your message. To paraphrase is not merely to parrot—to repeat mechanically what you have just said. Rather I want to show you that I have really heard *you*, that I have been present not just to your words but to their deeper meaning for you. I go beyond a simple assurance to you that I understand by offering you a statement of what I have understood. You can then confirm that, in fact, I have understood you—or clarify your message so that my understanding may be more accurate. In either case, I demonstrate my respect for you and for your message. It is important to me that I understand what you say, and it is to you that I come to check my understanding.

Empathy, then, is my ability to understand your ideas, feelings, and values from within your frame of reference. The goal of empathy is understanding; as such, it precedes evaluation. Empathy does not mean that I will always agree with you; it does not require that I accept your point of view as my own or even as the best one for you. I may well have to evaluate your ideas. We may well have to discuss and negotiate as we move toward a decision we can share. But these movements of evaluation and judgment come later in our communication. My first goal is accurately to understand you and what you are trying to say to me. Judgment and decision are not secondary in our communication, but they are subsequent to accurate understanding.

The open stance of empathy does much to enhance communication in settings of collaborative work or communal living. But communication involves more than receptivity. I must be able to speak as well as to listen; to initiate as well as to understand. Personal disclosure thus becomes an essential skill of community. In order to share my ideas or my concerns with you I must be able to overcome the hesitancy suggested by fear or doubt. But these inhibitions overcome, I must be able to act in a manner that enables you to know me in a way fitting for me and for our relationship. Appropriate self-disclosure can seem complicated. But I am not limited to my current level of success. I can become more skillful, learning better ways to express my values and needs, my ideas and feelings.

Appropriate self-disclosure begins in self-awareness. I must *know* what I have experienced, what I think, how I feel, what I need, what I want to do. This knowledge is not likely to be full and finished; an unwillingness to speak until I am completely sure of myself can be a trap in communication. Self-awareness is rather an ability to know where I am now, to be in touch with the dense and ambiguous information of my own life. Beyond knowing my own insights, needs, and purposes, I must value them. This need not mean that I am convinced that they are the best. It means rather that I take them seriously as deserving of examination and respect—from myself and from others as well. My ideas and feelings, my perceptions of myself and of the world—these have worth and weight. By valuing them myself I contribute to the possibility that they can be appreciated by others as well. My needs and purposes exist in a context of those of other people, to be sure. But a conviction that my own ideas and goals are of value is basic to mature self-disclosure.

An important skill of personal disclosure is my ability to speak concretely. I must be able to say "I," to acknowledge my own ideas and concerns. Self-disclosure can be thwarted by a retreat into speaking about "most people": "everybody knows . . ." instead of "I think that . . ."; "most people want . . ." instead of "I need . . ."; "people have a hard time . . ." instead of "it is difficult for me to . . ."

Beyond this willingness to own my experience, I can learn to provide more specific details about my actions and values and emotions. If we are to work effectively on a team, for example, it is important for me to be able to speak to you concretely about what I am doing and how I see this contributing to our common goal. As a lay person or a woman religious, I may need to develop my theological vocabulary so that I can more adequately describe my vision of the parish or my sense of myself as a minister. To share myself with friends or in a support group I will need a well-nuanced vocabulary of feelings—one that goes well beyond "I feel good" and "I feel bad." To tell you that "I feel good" is to share some important information about myself, but not yet very much. What does this mean for me? Is this good feeling one of confidence? or affection? or physical health? Does it result from something I have done or something that has been done for me? Are you an important part of this good feeling for me, or are you really incidental to it? In each of these instances my self-disclosure becomes more concrete when I can name my feelings more precisely and when I can describe the events and actions that are part of them for me.

Confrontation, too, makes a critical contribution to community. For most of us the word *confrontation* implies conflict. And as we shall see shortly, the ability to handle conflict is an important skill in community settings. But we use the word *confrontation* here in a meaning that goes beyond its narrow—and, most often, nega-tive—connotation as interpersonal conflict. The ability to confront involves the psychological strength to give (and to receive) emo-tionally significant information in ways that lead to further explo-ration rather than to self-defense. Sometimes the emotionally significant information is more positive than negative. To say "I love you" is to share with you emotionally significant information. And many of us know how confronting it is to learn of another's love for us. Similarly, to give a compliment is to share emotionally significant information, and there are people who defend them-selves against this "good news" as strongly as others of us defend ourselves against an accusation of blame. But most often, to be sure, when confrontation becomes necessary and difficult in com-munities, it is because there is negative information we must share.

Skills of confrontation are those behaviors that make it more likely that our sharing of significant negative information will lead us to explore the difficulty between us rather than to defend our-selves against one another. My ability to confront effectively is enhanced when I am able to speak descriptively rather than judg-mentally. To tell you that I missed an important meeting because you took the car and brought it back late is to *describe;* to call you a selfish and inconsiderate person is to *judge*. While both may be hard for you to hear from me, one is more likely to escalate into a quarrel than is the other. As we have noted before, judgment is not irrelevant in communication, but premature judgment is likely to short-circuit the process of exploration and mutual understand-ing. Perhaps there are extenuating circumstances that caused you to be late; perhaps you are genuinely sorry that you inconvenienced me and want to do something to make amends. My attack on you in calling you selfish is not likely to leave room for this kind of response on your side. It is more likely to lead you to defend yourself against my accusation, perhaps by calling up instances of my own selfishness, perhaps by leaving the scene altogether. In neither case has communication between us been furthered.

There are other behaviors that make our confrontation more effective, other behaviors more likely to further communication between us. These include the ability to accept feelings of anger in myself and in you and the ability to show respect for you even as I must disagree with you or challenge your position. These skills become especially important in dealing with conflict in community settings.

**Conflict and Community**

In talking about conflict as an aspect of Christian community, our rhetoric can be misleading. In our ceremonies and sermons we dwell upon images of unity and peace and joy. These images of life together as Christians are important and true, but partial. When, as a believing community, we do not speak concretely about the more ambiguous experiences of anger and frustration and misunderstanding in community life, we can leave many people confused and disappointed about their own relationships in groups.

Conflict and hostility are not goals of community, to be sure. But neither are they automatic indications that our parish or ministry team or religious house is in serious trouble. Conflict is both a normal and expected ingredient in any relationship—whether friendship or team work or family life—that brings people together and engages them at the level of their significant values and needs. Whenever persons encounter each other over a period of time— especially when matters of importance are involved—we can anticipate that differences will be noted, disagreements will develop, discord may emerge. The challenge in community relationships is not to do away with these signs of conflict or, worse, to refuse to admit them when they do arise. Rather we can attempt to learn to recognize the potential areas of conflict *for us* and to deal with these issues and feelings in ways that strengthen rather than destroy the bonds between us.

Conflict, then, is normal in interpersonal exchange; it can be expected in groups that function as communities. Communities engage us at the level of our significant concerns; groups that are communities are characterized by plurality as well as unity. The diversity inherent in community life can sometimes lead to an experience of discrepancy. And it is in response to discrepancy that conflict usually arises. This discrepancy can be in interpretation (we each give different meaning to the same event), in expectation (things have not turned out as I expected; you have not acted as I expected), or in need (I want you to be other than you are; I need the situation to be different than it is).

The presence of conflict between us can be an invitation to explore this discrepancy and thus to learn more about myself and about you. If we can discover the discrepancy to which our conflict points, we are in a better position to learn from it and to resolve it. But this opportunity for learning and for resolution is lost if we are unable to look into the conflict and turn instead to self-defense or to blame.

Conflict is more often a sign of a group's health than it is a symptom of disease. The presence of conflict among us most often indicates that we are involved in something we feel is significant— significant enough to generate the disturbances and tensions we are experiencing. Thus, conflict marks a relationship of some force. This energy can be harnessed; it need not always work against us. Groups in which there is nothing important enough to fight about are more likely to die than are groups in which some dissension occurs. Indifference is a greater enemy of community than conflict.

Conflict can be recognized as a step toward the resolution of tension, as an impulse whose aim is unity and peace. But this power of conflict is ambiguous. It can—and has, in the experience of most of us—led not toward unity and peace but toward increasing hostility and group disintegration. For many of us, it is these negative effects of conflict that we know best, and fear. Conflict feels bad: I am angry or hurt, you feel rejected or resentful. And beyond these bad feelings, conflict leads to the deterioration of relationships. Sometimes the relationship ends immediately; sometimes it continues, but with a burden of bitterness and unhealed grievances that ultimately leads to its death. In the face of this negative sense of the power of conflict, the evidence that it is expectable and even inevitable in community may strike me with alarm.

But these negative effects of conflict do not give the full picture. They are more likely to occur in groups where conflict is not anticipated, where its potential contribution is not understood, where attention has not been given to exploring the ways in which we can recognize and manage the discrepancies that arise among us.

## Facing Conflict

We may know from previous experience that conflict, faced poorly, can lead to resentment and recrimination. But failing to face it does not ensure that our community will be free of these negative emotions. An underlying problem seldom goes away because we refuse to face it. It may go underground for a while, but it is likely to reemerge later, with even more negative force. It is better to face the conflicts that may arise between us, aware of their ambiguous power both to damage and to deepen the relationships we share in this group. This willingness to accept conflict as inevitable—and even as potentially valuable—does not mean that we find it pleasant to be at odds. But it does mean that we are willing to acknowledge and even tolerate this discomfort that conflict brings, in view of the potential contribution that our diversity can make to our shared purposes.

The experience of facing together the conflicts that arise between us can give us a greater confidence in ourselves, an increased security in the strength and flexibility of the commitment between us, since we have seen it tested and found it sufficient to the test. Conflict can have this positive effect in a community, but it remains a powerful and ambiguous dynamic. Just as the presence of conflict does not necessarily or automatically signal a relationship in trouble, neither does it necessarily or automatically result in new learning or growth. Whether the presence of conflict in our group will have a positive or negative effect is due in large part to how we respond to it. To deal well with its ambiguous power, we must first appreciate the fact that conflict can be more than just negative among us. We must believe that the benefits of working through our conflict are worth the trouble and discomfort that attend. We must have the resources of personal maturity that enable us to face strong emotion and to look at ourselves anew and possibly change. And we must have the skills that enable us to deal effectively with one another even in the heat of our disagreement.

### Resolving Conflict

The ambiguous power of conflict is put at the service of our group through expectation, recognition, and management. For its positive potential to be harnessed for the community we must, first, *expect* that conflict will occur and that its occurrence will not be simply negative. There must be an awareness that conflict can be managed, that it can serve the purposes of the group. We can learn to *recognize* the ways in which conflict emerges among us—the issues or circumstances or exchanges by which it is evoked. We can agree, ahead of time, on some acceptable ways to deal with discrepancy and opposition when they do arise. We can hold ourselves and each other accountable to use these tools to *manage* conflict when it emerges among us. These tools of conflict management are varied, ranging from basic skills of clarification—such as paraphrasing and reflective listening—to more comprehensive strategies of problem-solving and negotiation. In the reference section at the end of this chapter we list some useful guides to these skills and strategies of conflict resolution in groups.

Thus, if our community is to flourish beyond the enthusiasm of its initial formation, it is important that we develop both a sense of the appropriateness—or at least the inevitability—of conflict and a common understanding of how we can deal with it. The methods we develop for conflict management can do more than forestall the disintegration of our group. They can be, as well, channels through which the rich diversity of the members is brought to awareness and, ultimately, put to the service of the community.

Conflict should not, of course, be the only—or the chief—experience of relationship in a group. A community must take care, especially at those points in its history when there is a good deal of conflict, to balance these experiences with expressions of a larger unity. Often this is achieved most effectively in ritual and celebration.

So we are brought back again to the importance of skills for community interaction. Those of us who participate in communities—especially those of us who minister to communities—can set out, even rather systematically, to acquire for ourselves and to encourage among others the skills that are helpful for life in community. Communication skills are needed: the ability to listen with accuracy and empathy to others; the ability to disclose information about myself, my needs and expectations, my own images and definitions of community—neither apologetically nor aggressively, but assertively. Skills of conflict resolution, negotiation, and problem-solving are essential to effectively incorporate diversity within community. Skills of empathy and imagination are needed to enable us to dream beyond the problem that seems to separate us and find a new solution in which we can stand together. And special skills are necessary for the celebration of both our diversity and our unity. These tools of community—skills of clarification, negotiation, imagination, celebration—are clearly not the whole story, especially when we speak of the building up of the community of faith. But skills can form an important chapter in the story of community, a chapter which is, perhaps, too often overlooked.

## FOR FURTHER REFLECTION

Take some time to consider your experience of communication and conflict in community settings. Begin in a mood of quiet, letting your memory turn back over the past year or so. Be attentive to the memories that come of the groups to which you belong. Spend time with this moment of recollection: let the memories come as they will, whether positive or negative, whether satisfying or unresolved.

From these several memories, choose one that is for you an instance of successful or satisfying communication in a community setting. Let this example come more fully to mind and then examine it more closely. In what ways was this experience satisfying for you? What was your own contribution to the success of the exchange? What did other people in the group contribute? How did you feel during the exchange? after?

Then turn to a memory of a difficult or unresolved exchange, perhaps a time of conflict in community. Again, consider the elements that were a part of the event. What was the focus of the difficulty? In what ways did your behavior (and that of others) add to the tension? In what ways did you (and others) try to resolve the problem? How did you feel during this exchange? after? What can you take from this experience to assist communication in community in the future?

## ADDITIONAL RESOURCES

Psychologist Gerard Egan has made significant contributions to the theory and practice of skills training. In *The Skilled Helper*, second edition (Monterey, CA: Brooks/Cole, 1981) Egan outlines a comprehensive program for training in the skills of effective communication and confrontation. In *You and Me: The Skills of Communicating and Relating to Others* (Monterey, CA: Brooks/Cole, 1977) he treats some of the same material in a simpler format, one that can be a valuable resource in programs with adults.

Thomas N. Hart offers an eminently practical look at skillful listening in the formal and informal settings of contemporary ministry in *The Art of Christian Listening* (New York: Paulist Press, 1981). In *The Assertive Christian* (Minneapolis: Winston Press, 1980) Michael Emmons and David Richardson discuss the skills of assertion in their relation to Christian values.

There are several considerations of conflict and confrontation available now that are of practical value as pastoral resources. In *Caring Enough to Confront* (Scottsdale, PA: Herald Press, 1980) David Augsberger examines the emotions that are a part of conflict and confrontation in a variety of interpersonal and ministerial contexts. Joseph E. Dittes offers guidelines for dealing with resistance and opposition within the community of faith in *When the People Say No: Conflict and the Call to Ministry* (San Francisco: Harper & Row, 1979). In his eminently readable style, Speed B. Leas treats both the expectability of conflict in parish life today and what lay persons can do to contribute to the successful resolution of this conflict in *A Lay Person's Guide to Conflict Management* (Washington, D.C.: The Alban Institute, 1981). John M. Miller, in *The Contentious Community: Constructive Conflict in the Church* (Philadelphia: Westminster Press, 1978), examines some of the normal polarities that are bound to create tension in the Church and discusses ways in which these tensions can contribute to the life of a congregation.

# 10 ✤
# Levels of Mutuality in Community Living
## Michael A. Cowan

The sense of community, of belonging to groups that respond to us as individuals worthy of dignity and respect, is rooted in the experience of mutuality. Mutuality refers to the ability of persons to engage in direct and nonmanipulative dialogue, each understanding and respecting the other's frame of reference. Relationships based on mutuality are lateral rather than vertical; they resemble friendship more than psychotherapy. When relationships among members of a group are characterized by mutuality, the opportunity for the experience of community in the group is enhanced. Mutuality within a community can occur at several levels. The differences in the levels of mutuality will depend on several factors: the goals of the group, the values members hold regarding personal sharing, even the operating rules that guide members' behavior toward one another. Critical to the experience of mutuality at any level will be the members' level of interpersonal skill.

### Self-Disclosure and Empathy
The first level of mutuality is characterized by two related behaviors: self-disclosure and empathy. Self-disclosure means the

*Michael A. Cowan* holds the doctorate in psychology from Ohio State University and is co-author of *People in Systems* and *Moving into Adulthood.* He is a founding member of Processus, a consultant group focussing on efforts to build effective human communities in educational, religious, and business settings. Previously he was on the staff of the Center for Human and Community Development and a member of the Department of Psychology at St. John's University in Collegeville, Minnesota. He currently offers courses in the university's School of Theology.

ability to share directly with another my feelings, thoughts, and values; empathy means the ability to hear accurately the thoughts, feelings, and values from another's frame of reference.

A relationship characterized by first-level mutuality is one in which the persons involved are willing to share their point of view in a conviction that they will be heard. This stance does not imply constant agreement. Rather, the norm of communication here is that each person listens and can expect to be listened to, irrespective of whether the parties agree or disagree. The initial attitude is one of attention; evaluation and decision are not necessarily secondary, but they are subsequent. Empathy and disclosure at this level are concrete ways in which people offer support to one another.

Just as this first level of mutuality does not necessarily imply agreement, neither does it necessarily imply emotional closeness. In many settings our communication is more about a common work than about our personal lives. And here, too, mutuality is critical. If we are to work together on a project, it is important that I can communicate directly to you my ideas, my feelings of enthusiasm or hesitation for the plan, my suggestions for changes and improvements. For us to collaborate effectively, it is important that you can see things from my point of view, not so that you can unquestioningly adopt my proposals, but so that you can more accurately assess their potential contribution. If we are unable to communicate directly with one another about the task, this lack of basic mutuality is likely to make our collaboration more difficult.

This first level of mutuality may be thought of as the minimal requirement for basic decency in human relationships. It provides a foundation for constructive communication in all social settings—family, classroom, religious community, or work place. A social setting that is not characterized by such basic decency in its patterns of communication is undermining rather than supporting the psychological health and development of its members by forcing them to defend themselves in order to avoid the risk of being hurt in group relationships. Empathy and disclosure are the foundation on which the succeeding levels of mutuality are built. The absence of these skills among members makes it difficult for groups to move toward deeper experiences of communication and community.

## Challenge and Self-Examination

It is the dynamic interplay of support and challenge that leads to the development of individuals and groups. If communities are to function developmentally, their communication must go beyond basic mutuality to include the possibility of responsible challenge. This challenge is characteristic of an intermediate level of mutuality. An essential form of developmental challenge involves the ability to invite another person to look constructively at issues, problems, or crises from a different frame of reference. The reciprocal behavior of this level of mutuality is self-examination. Self-examination depends on my willingness to receive the challenge as an invitation—an opportunity to look at myself or my position on an issue in a new light and to examine the possible validity of this alternate perspective.

Some examples may help to clarify the constructive interpersonal challenge that marks this second level of mutuality. Several members of a ministry team are concerned about another member's increasingly busy and harried work schedule. They have three basic options. They may ignore the behavior, or vent their feelings of irritation as they demand that the member act differently, or they may confront the person directly and responsibly. In another case, a principal becomes aware that racist or sexist attitudes are interfering with effective performance by an otherwise competent teacher. The options here parallel those of the ministry team: the principal may ignore the behavior; he or she may criticize the teacher and demand new behavior; or the teacher may be confronted directly and responsibly.

The limitations of the first response—ignoring the problem—are apparent. The individual loses an opportunity to receive information that may serve as the basis for positive developmental change. The setting suffers as well, since necessary tasks are not carried out or are carried out inadequately. The second option—to demand new behavior—is essentially a power tactic. It may elicit temporary compliance, but ultimately it leads to resistance and defensiveness on the part of the individual who is challenged in this manner. Moreover, this type of challenge is often experienced as an attack; it is likely to solidify the individual's position rather than to encourage self-examination and change. It may also complicate later communication, cluttering the relationship with negative emotions and issues that remain unresolved.

The third option—direct and responsible challenge—characterizes the second level of mutuality. It is important that such challenge be accompanied by empathy; as I confront another person I must communicate my awareness of and respect for her or his point of view. Confrontation needs to be understood and experienced by people as an *invitation* to examine some aspect of their behavior. Responsible challenge can be experienced as an invitation rather than an attack; it is thus likely to elicit exploratory rather than defensive responses. Not feeling that I am under attack, I experience less need to excuse or explain away my behavior. I may be able to look at myself in a new way, to try to examine my behavior in light of the new information I have received from you.

Not all relationships do or can move to this second level of mutuality. In some relationships this may be appropriate. But human relationships that are not open to responsible challenge are likely to remain limited and in some sense superficial. There is no development without adequate challenge. This holds true for groups as well as for individuals. Groups in which relationships among members operate consistently at the first level of mutuality may continue to function, even well. Such groups and relationships, however, are incomplete as developmental resources. Our personal and social development is enhanced when others are direct and responsible in sharing with us different ways of looking at things, and when we respond to these alternate perspectives with a willingness to examine ourselves and to change.

### Immediacy and Exploration of the Relationship

The second level of mutuality has an external focus. I invite you to examine your behavior, not as it directly affects me or our relationship but as it affects a larger value, task, or goal. The third level of mutuality has more limited scope. Here we focus on our relationship. Immediacy is the ability of individuals to share directly with one another information about aspects of their relationship that limit personal development or get in the way of collaborative action. To be an effective expression of mutuality, this immediacy must be complemented by a willingness to explore the relationship here and now.

The minister who experiences loneliness and resentment at being kept on a pedestal by the congregation, a teenager who feels that his own judgment is continually called into question by inflexible family regulations, a black supervisor who is afraid to comment on a white manager's insensitivity to potentially explosive racial issues, a lay woman in the parish staff who feels some of the pastor's demands are demeaning—all these are examples of immediacy concerns. Facing such issues directly and positively creates the potential for opening new areas of development to individuals and to the entire setting. Refusing to face them or facing them incompletely has the power to block such development.

Immediacy issues are potentially powerful sources of developmental change because of their highly personal nature; they deal directly with core issues of how *I* am experienced in a relationship: not merely my roles, tasks, or knowledge—but my *self.* Our ongoing development as persons is the result of events in the network of interpersonal relations that form the social settings of our lives. This fact gives foundation to the statement that mutuality in interpersonal relationships is critical to the development of persons and communities. Obviously, the depth and intensity of mutuality will differ with the type of setting. The intimacy of committed personal relationships is inappropriate in typical business relationships, but important interpersonal issues do arise and must be addressed even in such settings. No social setting—family, work place, parish, religious community, or classroom—can be fully effective if members cannot deal with one another appropriately at each of the three levels of mutuality discussed here.

## Factors Influencing Mutuality

If people are to involve themselves in relationships of mutuality, five interrelated factors must come into play: self-esteem, working knowledge, skills, values, and rules appropriate to the setting. The absence of any one of these factors is sufficient to account for a lack of mutuality in community living.

1. *Self-esteem.* The person with a very negative image of himself or herself is unlikely to risk the exposure and vulnerability that come with mutuality. While such a person may deeply desire close and meaningful relationships with others, the instinct for self-protection is likely to block efforts at intimacy. The lack of self-esteem in adult life may be related to problems of psychological development. It is important to note, however, that self-esteem can be low because a person perceives herself or himself to be lacking in basic interpersonal skills. In such instances, effective interper-

sonal skills training can lead to enhanced self-esteem; in other instances, the individual may be in need of psychological counseling in order to deal with the issue of self-image.

2. *Working knowledge.* Any information that helps me to behave competently in pursuing my goals can be termed working knowledge. In the case of interpersonal relationships, working knowledge is information that helps me to understand the behaviors that make up each level of mutuality as well as their relationship to each other. For example, research in psychology suggests that empathy, a behavior characteristic of first-level mutuality, has two distinct components: discrimination and communication. Discrimination refers to hearing accurately what another person is saying and how he or she seems to feel about it; communication means letting this other person know that I have heard accurately. Without *both* components, empathy is not present. This information becomes working knowledge when it helps me to understand empathy in my own life, when it influences my behavior.

3. *Skills.* A skill may be defined as a specific behavior or set of behaviors that can be engaged in by individuals at will and in the appropriate context. While working knowledge refers to what one knows, skills refer to what one can *do*. I may, for example, understand (working knowledge) the discrimination-communication distinction mentioned above. It does not follow, however, that I will be able to discriminate accurately the feelings and content contained in another's message (skill) or to communicate to this person that she or he has been understood (skill). Over the last decade, as we have seen in Chapter 9, a good deal of attention has been given to specifying those behaviors which best express and foster effective communication. Training programs in communication and other helping behaviors now exist, programs that can help people develop the skills associated with each of the levels of mutuality.

4. *Values.* A value may be defined as a chosen belief that actually influences my behavior. It may happen that people do not engage in effective and mutual communication, even when they seem to have the self-esteem, knowledge, and skills to do so. Members of a community may not establish among themselves relationships characterized by first-level mutuality (self-disclosure and empathy) even though it is not low self-esteem, ignorance of what such relationships entail, nor lack of skills that seem to be the cause. In such a case it is possible that the persons involved do not view

mutuality as a value. They may consider mutuality, in general, as a good idea, but it has not become a value for them since it does not influence their actual behavior. An early step in any effort to enhance mutuality within a community, then, must be a clarification of whether such mutuality is a shared value, one in which members are collectively willing to invest time and energy.

5. *Setting rules.* The final factor that effects the quality of mutuality within communities focuses not on what individuals bring to their relationships, but on the rules or norms of the setting in which the relationships occur. A religious house belonging to an order with a long tradition of interpersonal distance—the avoidance of intimacy—may find that these traditions and procedures based on them stand in the way of establishing relationships of mutuality as discussed here. A group with a strong tradition of work—serving others—may feel that time spent on developing relationships within the community itself takes time away from what is really important to them. Such rules can interfere with the development of relationships of mutuality in a community despite the presence of other factors that support mutuality. A community that wishes to expand levels of mutuality in its relationships should give attention to the norms and customs that guide behavior between members.

In attempting here to describe some aspects of the basic structure of mutuality, my approach has had a "how to" flavor about it. I have discussed practical ways in which we can assess the extent to which mutuality characterizes our dealings with each other and offered some concrete steps we can take to give mutuality a larger place in our day-to-day living in community. It seems appropriate to end my comments in a consideration of the "why" of mutuality— why should a Christian community concern itself with its corporate capacity to engage in relationships of mutuality?

My own response to this question takes the form of a brief set of propositions regarding the connection I see between the presence of mutuality in relationships and the psychological and spiritual development of human beings.

*Every act of authentic self-disclosure*
*makes one life a gift to the becoming of another.*
*Every act of accurate empathic understanding*
*enhances the listener's spirit.*

*Every act of responsible challenge in the spirit of
empathy is an invitation to an increase in stature.*

*Every act of non-defensive exploration in response
to challenge reflects a commitment to a life
of larger dimensions.*

Anyone who struggles to develop the tenderness, discipline, and resilience of spirit that such giving and receiving demand knows at firsthand both the moments of dying entailed and the intensity of living that can result. To care for one another and to accept one another's care in this spirit of deep mutuality is to place our ordinary acts of face-to-face interaction in community within the ultimate context of love.


## FOR FURTHER REFLECTION

Examine these levels of mutuality in the communities in which you participate. Select a particular group and consider your experience over the last year or so.

1. Find examples of events or exchanges that represent first-level mutuality: self-disclosure and empathy. What factors or circumstances contribute to the development of this quality of mutuality within this group?

2. Look for examples of second-level mutuality: responsible challenge and self-examination. Then consider what might be done to help further develop these expressions of mutuality in this group.

3. Have you experienced third-level mutuality: immediacy and exploration of the relationship? Are there factors that help group members reach this level of mutuality? Are there factors that stand in the way of this level of mutuality in the group?


## ADDITIONAL RESOURCES

In *People in Systems* (Monterey, CA: Brooks/Cole, 1979) Gerard Egan and Michael Cowan draw from a variety of the social sciences to provide a practical, helpful framework for understanding the ways in which people participate in the systems that make up their social lives. See, especially, their discussion in Chapter 11, "Toward Mutuality in Human Systems." Egan's earlier work, *Interpersonal Living* (Monterey, CA: Brooks/Cole, 1976) is a comprehensive look at the kinds of behavior that contribute concretely to the experience of mutuality between persons. For another approach to skills development in communities, see John McKinley's *Group Development through Participant Training* (New York: Paulist Press, 1980).

In *The Future of Partnership* (Philadelphia: Westminster Press, 1979), Letty Russell challenges Christian communities to take seriously the gospel call to radical mutuality. In *Mutual Ministry* (New York: The Seabury Press, 1977) James Fenhagen sees the experience of reconciliation as essential in the building and sustaining of communities in which mutual ministry may develop.

# 11 ✤
# Community in the Life
# of the Minister

The communal dimensions of ministry have received new attention in the Roman Catholic Church since Vatican II. Developments in theology, in the forms of religious experience and expression, and in the structures of parishes, religious congregations, and the diocesan priesthood have emphasized the corporate elements of the Christian mission. As a result, three kinds of social groupings are likely to be a part of the expectation and the experience of persons in ministry today. These groupings are support networks, residential communities, and teams in ministry. There is some ambiguity, even confusion, regarding these terms and the realities in our lives to which they refer. The terms are sometimes used as synonyms, as though each referred to the same kind of group, the same quality of interpersonal experience. Both experience and analysis, however, suggest that this is not the case.

*Support network*, *residential community* and *ministry team* are terms that designate three quite distinct social groupings. Each has its own particular objectives, its own dynamics, its own pressures and rewards. Each can make a valuable contribution to the vitality of the Christian minister. But the three are not equivalent concepts. And, most often, they will not be the same in one's experience. There is a tendency among Catholic ministers to consider the same group of persons as one's support group, one's community, and one's ministry team. It is not impossible that the identical group of persons will be able to function adequately for one another as principal sources of personal support, as a visible community of shared values and life style, and as an effective context for collaborative action. It is not impossible, but it is not easy.

An initial distinction can be made among these three group entities in terms of principal or originating focus. A principal focus of a personal support network is *I*, the self. A chief focus of the community is *we*, the visible collectivity of persons. And an orienting focus of the team in ministry is *task*, the job to be done. This way of distinguishing these groupings from one another is, obviously, too simple. But it may serve as a first step in clarifying these different forms of social experience.

### Personal Support Network

My personal support network is made up of those persons whose presence, support, and challenge enable my personal and professional life to flourish. We speak of a *support network* rather than a *support group*. A group generally refers to persons who are all in relationship with one another. There may well be a support group in my life—several people who all know each other and interact together on a regular basis for mutual encouragement and growth. But the sources of support for my personal and professional life will extend beyond such a group to include persons who have particular relationships with me, but are not related in a group with one another. Many of us, for example, have looked forward to introducing to each other two persons who are each important to us, only to find that these two have no real basis for friendship between themselves. In this instance both of these friends may be part of my support network, though the three of us do not, precisely speaking, constitute a support group.

My close friends will form an important part of my support network; some members of my family are likely to be important here as well. But the network will also include persons whose relationship with me does not have the mutuality of family ties or close friendship. For example I may develop an ongoing relationship with a spiritual director, a person who assists me in my efforts to discern and to respond to the movements of God in my life. This relationship may be critical to my development as a person of faith and as a minister, yet the person who is of assistance to me in this way need not be a close personal friend. There are other persons, resources for my professional life, who are important in my support network and yet are not personal intimates or close friends. Colleagues in ministry and professional peers in my area of specialization are sources of information, encouragement, and critique, supporting my development as a competent minister. At particular points in my career I may seek regular contact with a personal supervisor who will assist my efforts to improve my ministerial effectiveness. At other times I may benefit from discussions with a psychological counselor. Each of these are instances of the kinds of relationships that constitute a personal support network.

In two senses I am the focus of my personal support network. First, and most obviously, it is my needs that give shape to the network. This statement can be disconcerting. It can seem narcissistic and appear to contradict the call to selfless service that should characterize ministry. But there is, increasingly, among religious persons the realization that personal development is neither irrelevant to nor distracting from one's life with God. The quality of ministry depends in large part (as the experience of the Church has shown) upon the quality of its ministers. And most of us sense, even more immediately, that our own effectiveness in ministry is directly related to the level of our spiritual, intellectual, and emotional development. Attention must be given to continuing growth in each of these areas. Careful attention can begin in an appreciation of both my native strengths and my current needs. My strengths and my needs—in areas of friendship, prayer, and ministry—will give shape to my network of personal support. This analysis of strengths and needs will reveal the who and how of my current support network; it will provide indications of ways in which this network should be expanded or changed.

This brings us to the second sense in which I am the focus of my personal support network. The responsibility for developing and maintaining such a network of supportive relationships falls largely upon the individual. More and more there is a realization among religious persons that the principal agent in one's adult life is, under God, oneself. Earlier forms of spirituality and religious discipline, those that seem to reinforce dependency and passivity, are judged less appropriate to the demands of a contemporary asceticism. I am responsible for developing in my life those relationships which challenge me beyond mediocrity and support my continuing development as a faithful and vital Christian minister.

## Residential Community

For many in ministry, as we have noted before, the first sense of *community* is the local house of the religious congregation. But community has a broader meaning today as a goal in personal life and as an objective in ministry. There is among many in ministry the desire to be a part of an identifiable group with whom one shares the significant values and important purposes of one's life. A *we* focus is central to this desire for community—whether the *we* is visible as a local residence (convent, rectory, commune) or as a group that is identifiable in some other way (a prayer group or parish committee or the core members of a more loosely defined movement, such as the prison reform movement, the women's movement, the right-to-life movement). In our discussion now, however, we will focus on the experience of residential community.

The hope of living with others in Christian community is no longer an expectation of vowed religious alone. Today there are groups of laypersons and of diocesan priests, as well as religious women and men, who are concerned that their local residences be true communities. This goal is important to them both for its contribution to their own lives and for its importance as a witness to the gospel promise of life among Christians. In more and more instances, the religious residence is not simply a place to which one is assigned on the basis of need, without prior consultation. Increasingly, those who live together have some choice in regard to residence and some influence regarding the life style of the houses in which they live. And increasingly, these religious persons are determining that their residences are to be more than convenient places to live in order that their work may be accomplished.

Christians today are demanding that life together be characterized by more significant signs of community than joint membership or common residence. Most frequently this request for more is expressed in terms of some sharing in faith experience and some expectations of personal support. The development of each of these added dimensions will require time and creative attention within a community. There is a strong desire among most religious persons to be able to share their spiritual journey in shared prayer and communal worship. This desire can be experienced very acutely today. In this time of profound religious transition and shifting cultural norms, there can be wide divergence regarding the forms of prayer and faith-sharing that are preferable, or even acceptable. In an atmosphere of flexibility and tolerance, such diversity can be experienced as enriching. But in many instances this experience of diversity in religious values or expression has functioned destructively in a group. The development of appropriate forms of communal prayer must be undertaken with sensitivity to this diversity and to the recent and sometimes painful history of change within the Church. But this effort must be undertaken. The growth of community life among religiously motivated persons will be dependent, in significant part, upon its success.

The expectation that there will be a shared experience of personal support among members is common in residential communities today. This does not mean that only close friends can live together. Friendship and community are not synonyms. Neither are they antonyms, of course. In many ways, the more persons who are members of a community (residential or otherwise) like each other, the better it is. But the value of friendship is only one of the values around which communities may form. Many may find that a common commitment to justice, or to quality education for the poor, or to affirming the religious significance of suffering, is of sufficient personal meaning to sustain them in community with persons who share that value commitment but who are not close personal friends. That is not to suggest that the quality of personal exchange in such communities must—or can be allowed to —disintegrate to a level of polite anonymity. As we have seen earlier, opportunities for personal exchange and for the expression of personal support are key characteristics of those groups which function as communities. But the range of expressions of personal support and mutual concern is wide. As a person's range of interpersonal experience broadens, he or she becomes aware of the many nuances of friendship and care and of the variety of their appropriate expression. The personal experience of many religious and priests has broadened over the past decade to include friendship with persons outside their congregations and the ranks of the diocesan clergy. These experiences have contributed to an apreciation of the many ways in which the gift of personal concern is offered and received. Drawing upon this added interpersonal sophistication, residential communities can be better prepared to devise suitable opportunities for members to communicate with each other at a personal level and to share expressions of mutual concern and care.

**Team Ministry**

An originating focus of the teams that are increasingly a part of the Church's experience today is the task of ministry. In the logic of team ministry, persons come together in order to accomplish corporately a task that they could not achieve—or could not achieve as well—alone. In this understanding, the central questions that are to be raised in regard to the team, its composition, and its activities are "does this facilitate the task?"; "does this promote our ministry?"

The response to these questions can be somewhat complicated, since the circumstances of most ministry teams are complex. It can be argued, for example, that witness to the possibility of caring relationships among people is central to all Christian ministry. Thus, *community*, in some meanings of the term, becomes an integral part of the *task* of the ministry team. Nevertheless, it remains useful to this analysis to consider the team-in-ministry as a form of social interaction that can be distinguished from both *"residential community"* and *"support network."*

The complexity of team ministry is seen again in the variety of motives that influence the decision to participate in a team. Many persons seek out the team context in a conviction that joint action can accomplish what individual effort cannot ("In a group we can accomplish more than any of us can alone."). Coordinated planning and collaborative action are likely to characterize ministry teams that share this conviction.

Other teams have developed with the explicit goal of providing mutual support and encouragement among persons engaged in difficult and frustrating ministries. In these instances, coordinated planning and joint action may be secondary to the more pervasive goal of sustaining one another in the midst of arduous and demanding tasks. Clusters formed among inner-city parishes and alliances established among persons in justice ministries are often teams in this sense. For some, the move toward team ministry is guided by the theological conviction that Christian ministry is always a communal activity, that it can never be done alone. For these persons, the witness provided by the ongoing effort to work together in honesty and respect stands at the core of the good news that Christians have to share with modern women and men.

Any one person's involvement in team ministry is likely to be influenced by some combination of these reasons, as well as others. The job that is available, one's previous experience in both autonomous and cooperatie ministry, an awareness of personal strengths and limitations—these are all factors that weigh in the decision to join or to remain with a team. This complexity of motives is the rule rather than the exception, and frequently leads to complications in the functioning of the team. It is not easy to achieve simultaneously several different goals of team membership. The demands of the shared task may dominate the team, crowding out the time that is necessary for mutual support and critique. A commitment to proceed on consensus decision-making may delay effective action. Actions taken to achieve one goal of team interaction will not automatically contribute to other goals. In fact, some actions may help a team in one area and yet cause problems in another. A program of performance evaluation may contribute to the achievement of the team's shared task and yet foster a destructive sense of competition among members. Time spent in personal sharing and mutual support will increase the team's sense of cohesion, but may divert energies away from the external challenges that the group must meet. A team that intends several goals— collaboration in ministry, mutual encouragement and critique, communal witness—should be aware that each of these factors has its own set of requirements. Attention must be paid to each. These complications do not suggest that team ministry is impossible; but they are a sobering reminder of the complexity of human collaboration.

It is not impossible for the same cluster of persons to function for each other as support group, residential community, and team in ministry. It is not impossible, but neither is it easy. As we have seen, each group form makes its own particular demands on members. And these differing demands can be experienced as contradictory. My commitment to support you through a difficult time in your personal life may conflict with my commitment to meet a critical challenge in our shared ministry. A group assumes many responsibilities when its members choose to be for one another visible community, personal support network, and ministry team. There are clear advantages to a situation that enables persons to live and work with good friends, but there are inherent strains as well. Such a group will undoubtedly experience, from time to time, the antagonism inherent in its multiple responsibilities to one another. Many religious groups are unprepared for this. These strains are interpreted not as a normal and expected aspect of a complex undertaking, but as an indication of group weakness or individual selfishness.

The situation is even more difficult when the group has not come to an explicit awareness of the range of goals and purposes among its members. Members may have differing images of what the group is about, differing expectations of how members should be related to one another. This diversity is to be expected, particularly in the initial stages of a group's life. But difficulties are likely to develop if these differences in image and expectation are not recognized and resolved.

Clarification is a starting point in the effort to understand the multiple purposes that bring people together in groups. Compromise, the effort to reach a satisfactory resolution of differences, is a continuing dynamic of group life. It is a part of planning and problem solving as well as of friendship and support. The dual process of clarification and compromise will be an indispensable element of any group's attempt to discern its various obligations and to mediate the legitimate demands to which these give rise. Christian ministry is a corporate undertaking. An awareness of the diversity of group forms and a respect for the power and limit of each can contribute to the vitality of ministry and the creativity of the minister.

## FOR FURTHER REFLECTION

To what extent are these three social groupings a part of your own life?

1. Who are the persons who make up your own network of personal support?

2. Do you participate in "a visible grouping of shared value and purpose"? Who is with you in this community? Is it a residential community?

3. Are you a part of a team in ministry? Who are the members of the team?

Chart the areas of overlap, noting the persons who appear in more than one of these groupings.

4. What are the positive effects of this overlap—the ways in which your relationship or your work is enhanced?

5. Are there any negative effects of this overlap—ways in which your relationship or work is complicated?

ADDITIONAL RESOURCES

The ongoing Seminar on Jesuit Spirituality has considered questions of residential religious community. See, for example, Michael J. Buckley's discussion, "Mission in Companionship," in the September 1979 issue of *Studies in the Spirituality of Jesuits* and "Living Together in Mission" by P.J. Henriot, J.A. Appleyard, and J.L. Klein, in the March 1980 issue. Valuable analyses of various aspects of residential religious community appear regularly in *Sisters Today, Review for Religious,* and *Sojourners.* For a theological discussion of community life as a part of the experience of vowed religious today, see Francis J. Moloney, *Disciples and Prophets: A Biblical Model for the Religious Life* (New York: Crossroad Publishing Co., 1981) and David Fleming, "Community, Corporateness and Communion" in *Starting Points,* a 1980 publication of the Contemporary Theology Project sponsored by the Leadership Conference of Women Religious. Rosine Hammett and Loughlin Sofield discuss the dynamics of residential communities in *Inside Christian Community* (New York: Le Jacq Publishing, 1981).

In *Developing Support Groups* (San Diego: University Associates, 1978), Howard Kirschenbaum and Barbara Glaser offer helpful guidelines for forming groups of mutual support and enrichment, along with a discussion of several of the most common problems that can emerge over the life of these groups. The notion of the support group is broadened considerably by Phyliss Silverman in *Mutual Help Groups: Organization and Development* (New York: Sage Publications, 1980).

Naomi I. Brill looks at the internal and external life of collaborative work groups in *Teamwork: Working Together in the Human Services* (New York: Lippincott, 1976). William Gordon and Roger Howe consider the strategies through which teams are built and nourished in *Team Dynamics in Developing Organizations* (Dubuque: Kendall/Hunt, 1977). Dody Donnelly's discussion of the theory and practice of team functioning is available in *Team* (New York: Paulist Press, 1979).

# ❖ PART V

# FORMING THE COMMUNITY OF FAITH

# 12 ❖

# Ministering to the Sense
# of the Faithful

Christian communities are neither neutral sites where individual Christians exercise their faith, nor are they merely the passive objects of ministry. A maturing faith community is itself generative of faith. Whether a parish, religious congregation, school, or diocese, a Christian community can be expected to become a source of religious insight and ministry. As a group matures, it comes into its own vocation and special ministry: more confident in its Christian values and resources, it becomes better able to witness and minister to the society in which it lives and to the Church of which it is a member.

If this generative aspect of community life excites us, we are also aware that it takes time for such maturity to develop. How does a group of believers come to a sense of their faith and an awareness of how, specifically, they are to express this faith in their lives? One avenue for exploring both the generative nature of a faith community and its religious maturing is in terms of the traditional category of the sense of the faithful.

**The Sense of the Faithful**

The root insight of this notion of a sense of the faithful (*sensus fidelium*) is that the Christian Church—and so, each community of believers—possesses an intuitive sense, an instinct about Christian faith and living.[1] This trustworthy sense of belief must be related

---

1. Two related Latin phrases are found in theological discussions of this category: *sensus fidei*, a "sense of faith" and *sensus fidelium*, a "sense of the faithful." Both refer to a feeling for Christian faith that belongs to believers. At different times in our religious history, popes and theologians have turned to the notion of a "sense of faith" that abides in the Church and on which we can depend. In the nineteenth

to the indwelling of the Spirit, the continuing presence of God in our midst. In this chapter we will ask a number of practical questions about this sense of belief. Traditionally the sense of the faithful has been understood as belonging to the *whole* Church. How is this universal sense rooted in the practical, developing faith of individual communities of faith?

A second question concerns the infallible nature of the Church's sense of faith. How is this unerring sense of belief—better, this trustworthy intuition about our faith—related to our pluralistic experience of lived faith? If a universal agreement about our faith is grounded in the sense of faith alive in many faith communities, then we must leave room for plural "senses" of belief as these many Christian communities struggle toward the ideals of consensus and agreement.

If we can relate this rhetorical "sense of the faithful" to the practical life of specific communities (a goal of this chapter), then we may be able to chart the religious maturing of a community according to the formation of its own trustworthy sense of faith. The maturity of a community of faith will be related to its developing sense or instinct about Christian values and how these are to be practically lived. Each community might be expected to come into a practical and reliable sense of how to exercise its faith—how we as Christians here and now are to celebrate the Lord's presence, to act for justice, to commit ourselves in love and work. This practical sense of belief is fragile and always in need of development: as such it is a focus of the ministry to a community. And it is a sense of faith that is rooted in the whole body of believers. It is not a set of teachings or beliefs brought to the community by professional ministers, but a sense or instinct about lived faith that is developing within this body of believers. It is, in more traditional vocabulary, the conscience of this community, the corporate conscience of this group of Christians, most of whom are not clergy but laity.

---

century, for example, Cardinal Newman argued that the growth of Christian faith is rooted in an abiding and often inarticulate "sense" that the faithful possess. Pope Pius XII, in 1954, asserted that the dogmatic definition of the Blessed Virgin's assumption into heaven was a proclamation of a belief that had until then been abiding in "the sense of belief that belongs to the Christian people." In the statements of the Second Vatican Council, the characteristics of the Church's sense of faith are universality (agreement among "the people as a whole") and inerrancy (the Church's infallible relationship to faith). Later in this chapter, we shall explore the use that Newman and the documents of the Second Vatican Council make of this theological category.

### Instincts, Feelings, and Faith

The sense of the faithful obviously refers to sensibility and feeling; it also suggests intuitions and instincts. But all of these words can cause uneasiness in many Christians. Is not our Christian faith precisely that kind of conviction that rescues us from mere feelings? Is not faith a certainty that liberates us from the moods and impulses that sometimes threaten to overturn our lives? For many of us in our psychologically sensitive culture, instinct and intuition suggest dark inclinations rooted in unconscious biological drives. Our instincts, especially those touching on sexuality and anger, seem to be intimately linked to our sinfulness and inhumanity. Should not religious maturity mean deliverance from these impulsive forces?

In the realm of faith, many of us have been taught to be especially cautious about feelings. We have learned to understand faith as an intellectual assent to God's saving presence in life; as such it does not depend on feelings or senses or instincts. Feelings may thus seem alien to both belief and moral action. We judge our instincts to be suspect, much more likely to lead us to do what we feel like than what we ought to do.

Often, then, a healthy hesitancy about feelings and instincts has led to an unhealthy mistrust of them. But many of us today are being invited back to a religious involvement with our feelings. The invitation comes from our experience of both love and worship. We find that we cannot love only rationally. Our commitments of love—in marriage, religious community, friendship—necessarily involve feelings and instincts as well. Our life choices—to marry this person or follow this career—are never merely intellectual assents or clear and rational decisions. We marry this person at this point in our life not because we ought to, or because this choice is rationally correct. We marry because after much reflection we sense that this is a good decision. We learn quickly that loving well demands highly refined and well-formed instincts; graceful loving requires not a separation from, but a forming of our feelings according to our deepest Christian values and hopes.

Likewise in our liturgical life: we cannot, do not want to, celebrate in a simply rational fashion. Feelings, shaped by song and movement and costume and incense, guide and enhance our celebration of God's presence in our lives. Worship reminds us of the centrality of feelings in Christian life; our liturgies contribute powerfully to the shaping and maturing of our feelings and instincts.

Despite, perhaps, our earlier suspicions about feelings, as we mature we come to see that we cannot live without them. We recognize that religious growth does not mean deliverance from feeling, but involves the *forming* of human feelings according to Christian values and hopes.

What does the New Testament tell us about Christian ways of feeling? Do instincts shaped by Christian faith differ from other ways of feeling? Perhaps the most illuminating term in the New Testament presentation of Christian instincts is the Greek word *phronein*, "to sense." Jerome, in his translation of the New Testament, chose the Latin word *sapere* to convey this way of feeling. Both the Greek and Latin words mean "to sense or feel," but may also be translated as "to be sensible." The noun form of *sapere* is *sapientia*, wisdom. In these words of the New Testament is suggested a development of human instincts: as our senses mature, we not only "sense" things, but become sensible and sensitive; such sensitivity leads, in turn, to prudence and wisdom.

**Figure 12.1**

---

### THE MATURING OF HUMAN INSTINCTS

| *to sense, feel* | *to be sensitive, sensible* | *to be wise, astute* |
|---|---|---|
| Gr: *phronein* | *phronein* | *phronimos* (prudent) |
| Lt: *sapere* | *sapere* | *sapiens* (wise) |
| (the basic ability to feel, taste, smell) | (a maturing ability to savor, "be in touch with") | (a matured, reliable sense of how to act) |

---

The word *phronein* appears in a number of contexts in the New Testament, often disguised in its various English translations.[2] The well-known parable of the ten virgins in Matthew 25 distinguishes

2. The word appears most frequently in Paul's letters, especially Romans and Philippians. It does not appear in the fourth gospel; among the synoptics, the word is most used by Matthew.

The wide range of meanings and nuances of this word is suggested in its many translations in the New Testament. The full force of its "feeling" connotations is

between the five who were foolish (not being prepared to wait for the late-arriving bridegroom) and the five who were "sensible." Being sensible means sensing how to act, having the formed feelings that lead to effective action. In the gospel of Luke we encounter another, more confusing parable; a dishonest steward, about to be fired by his employer, makes friends with his employer's debtors by reducing their obligations. His employer, on firing him, also praises him for his "astuteness"(Lk.16:8). It is the Greek *phronein* that appears here as astuteness—the ability or "good sense" to act a certain way in this situation. The same word appears again in the account of Jesus commissioning his disciples; as he sends them out into the world, Jesus encourages them "to be *cunning* as serpents and yet as harmless as doves" (Mt. 10:16). Sensible, astute, cunning—the ability that comes from highly developed instincts and enables one to act effectively in different situations. Beyond these uses of *phronein* in the New Testament, it is useful to examine the three passages in which the term is used to make more explicit the meaning of a Christian way of feeling.

In Chapter 16 of Matthew's gospel (and its parallel in Mark 8) Jesus is preparing to go up to Jerusalem. He feels that he must do this although he also senses that this move could lead to great danger and even death. Peter objects to this plan and argues that Jesus should not go to Jerusalem. The two men clearly have different feelings about what is to be done. Jesus, suddenly angered, utters one of his most emphatic statements: "Get behind me, Satan. You are an obstacle in my path because you do not *sense* the things of God, but those of men" (Mt. 16:23). Peter's way of feeling, his instinctive response—that Jesus not take a chance in going to Jerusalem, not follow this inner urging which might make him vulnerable to danger—is opposed to "feeling the things of God."

---

evident in Paul's affectionate statement to the Christians of Philippi that "it is only natural that I should *feel* like this toward you all" (Phil. 1:7). Later in this letter appears the familiar injunction: "In your minds you must be the same as Christ Jesus" (Phil. 2:5). A better translation might be "in your sensibilities and feelings." To be of like mind is also to be of like heart, similar inclinations and feelings. Finally, a third meaning of *phronein*, still in the letter of the Philippians, is that of judgment. The sinful and worldly, Paul observes, "*think important* the things of the world" (Phil. 3:19). In his letter to the Romans, Paul would "urge each one among you not to *exaggerate* his real importance. Each of you must *judge* himself soberly . . ." (Rom 12:3). To exaggerate is to overestimate (*hyper-phronein*). Judging is prudent and wise when it arises out of accurate and matured sensibilities.

The intent of the following reflection is to recapture the intuitive and feeling aspects of this New Testament word.

Peter has followed his instincts, but the wrong ones; he has responded in a seemingly "sensible" way, but in a way that Jesus finds unholy. In his decision to go to Jerusalem, Jesus is following his own instincts, but they are also the "instincts of God"—a sense of how to act that has been formed by his attentiveness to his Father.

A reader may well miss this opposition of sensibilities in Matthew's gospel. This is because the feeling connotation of *phronein* is lost or disguised in many English translations. In the Jerusalem Bible this phrase in Matthew 16:23 is translated: "The way you think is not God's way, but man's." In the Oxford Revised Standard translation, all sensing disappears in "You are not on the side of God, but of men." Putting more "feeling" into the translation of this passage better emphasizes Jesus' assertion that there is "a godly way of sensing" that is quite different from our more ordinary sensibilities. We can become aware of this practically in our own struggles to act as mature Christians. As I come to an important life choice (for example, whether to change the direction of my career) I scrutinize my motives and the feelings and instincts that are leading me to this choice. Does this growing "sense" of what I should do arise from selfishness or cowardice? Or is it rooted in an attentive listening to God's guidance in my life? An important moment in religious maturity comes in my recognition of the trustworthiness of my feelings. This is a gradually accrued confidence, developed over decades of Christian living, that I can trust my instincts because they are of God.

A second passage which distinguishes a mature Christian way of sensing appears at the end of Paul's first letter to the Corinthians. Describing the different stages of religious maturity, Paul turns to the metaphor of human development:

> When I was a child, I used to talk like a child, *feel* like a child and argue like a child, but now I am a man, all childish ways are put behind me (1 Cor. 13:11).

Again we encounter an opposition of two ways of behaving, rooted in different ways of feeling. Adult maturity entails the letting go of childish ways of feeling, or more accurately, the transformation of these ways of feeling as they become more trustworthy resources.

Again a "way of feeling" is disguised in many English translations of this passage. Both the Jerusalem Bible and the Oxford
Revised Standard translate this phrase "to think like a child."
However, the Good News for Modern Man edition of the New Testament does recapture the sense of *phronein* in its translation:
"When I was a child, my speech, *feelings* and thinking were all
those of a child." Unfortunately, this interest in feeling may be
traced to the context of childhood. This edition's translation of
Matthew 16:23 as "These *thoughts* of yours are not of God but of
men" suggests that the translators were more comfortable ren-
dering *phronein* as feeling when it referred to childhood—the domain of feeling as opposed to rational adulthood. By more
accurately restoring some "feeling" to this passage, we recover an
awareness of Christian maturity that is very much concerned with
feelings and instincts.

Paul's most emphatic statement about Christian feelings appears
in his letter to the Romans. In Chapter 8, Paul makes the famous
distinction between "those who live according to the flesh" and
"those who live according to the Spirit" (Rom. 8:5). The first group
"set their minds on the things of the flesh"; the others "set their
minds on the things of the Spirit." "Set their mind" is the Oxford
Revised Standard translation of *phronein*. (The Jerusalem Bible
translates the Greek verb here as "are interested in.") The meaning
of this word encompasses all one's feelings and inclinations. As
Ernst Kaesemann has observed in his *Commentary on Romans*,
"*Phronein* denotes the direction not merely of thought but of total
existence." But the feeling aspect of this personal inclination is
disguised in the cerebral translations of many English texts. A
more faithful translation of this passage might be "set their hearts
on" or even "are attuned to" the things of the Spirit.

Whatever the translation, in these passages in Matthew, 1 Corinthians, and Romans we meet a distinction between styles of feeling and action. Ways of sensing that are worldly, childish, and
fleshly are distinguished from ways of feeling that are godly, mature, spiritual. How shall we understand this maturing of our feelings and instincts that identifies us as mature Christians?

## Christian Maturity: The Seasoning of Instincts

To better understand how a community matures into a confident
sense of faith, it is useful to recall the ways in which personal

maturity includes the formation and transformation of feelings. We have argued that Christian maturity entails not the banishment of our senses and instincts, but their shaping according to the values of Jesus Christ.

In our reflection on feelings and instincts, we do well to recall that human instincts—whether concerning sexuality or safety or power or even food—are never "raw instincts." As the anthropologist Claude Lévi-Strauss has suggested, our instincts are always cooked—that is, influenced by our environment. We never find ourselves with pure, uninfluenced inclinations and aspirations. The values and biases of our society and neighborhood and family have, from the beginning of our lives, been shaping our feelings and ways of responding. Our ways of reacting to other people, to authority, to sexual stimuli are never simply spontaneous, but are carefully— if often unconsciously—learned from life around us. (If human instincts are never raw, there are those whose feelings and ways of reacting are not only cooked but marinated, even pickled. Too thoroughly influenced and shaped by external forces, such people have lost their spontaneity and liveliness.)

An image that may capture the proper maturing of our feelings and instincts in that of *seasoning*. Growing up in a Christian family and participating in the life of a parish, we learn gradually over many seasons how Christians respond. We watch how others whom we cherish act. We learn their intuitive sense of how Christians treat their own bodies, how they are present to those whom they love. We observe how Christians feel about others—the poor, the sexually marginal, those who speak other languages and display different cultural habits. We learn over the years how Christians celebrate: what kind of events bring this group to celebration, how their minds and hearts and bodies are brought to worship.

Christian maturing is the seasoning of instincts. In unconscious as well as conscious ways, our feelings are gradually formed by Christian values and hopes. Christian communities provide both the context and the examples for this formation of feelings. And, of course, as with every human and religious effort, we often fail at this formation. A family or parish may itself be unchristian in some aspect of its own maturity—displaying an unholy distrust of the body or an outright rejection of some others who are mistakenly judged not to be of God's family. The young in such communities are shaped and seasoned in these unchristian ways. The challenge of Christian formation and education is to learn to provide the proper seasoning.

This image of seasoning has within it a number of important elements. Obviously, it includes the notion of an external influence: the environment and atmosphere in which we grow up is shaping us. Second, seasoning suggests considerable duration: the shaping of our feelings and intuitions about justice and sex and friendship and forgiveness takes many seasons. Over several decades our sense of how to respond in different situations is formed by the values and hopes that are the milieu of our life. It is only gradually and with many reversals, failures, and confusions that we become seasoned Christians. *Seasoned* also suggests being both "familiar with" and "good at." We have been at it sufficiently long that we know, intuitively, how to respond; we know, now often without complex or arduous reflection, how we as Christians are to respond in this situation.

Another important part of the image of being seasoned as a Christian is that the values of Jesus Christ have seeped all the way through us. No longer a simply external authority or set of values, they have been internalized and personalized. They have become us. To describe this transformation of our feelings and ways of sensing is to say that we have been *Christianized*. Here the word does not refer to the event of our formal entrance into the Church; it refers to the inner shaping of how we feel and act by the values of Jesus Christ.

The result of this seasoning (which is itself always continuing since we are never fully and finally matured) is that our instincts become trustworthy. Never infallible, they do become, in time, reliable. The mature Christian is one whose feelings—about when and how to express anger or affection, about who is my neighbor—are trustworthy. Shaped and seasoned by Christian values, our instincts become dependable. Our feelings are transformed so that we experience them neither as alien nor as simply unpredictable. They become positive resources in our life, part of an inner authority whose movements we can trust. Thus, we mature in our faith life as we learn to consult and trust the authority of our seasoned instincts.

We recognize here an important strength of Christian adulthood. With these inner resources to rely on, we are less susceptible to the worldly forces that would seduce us. Or, in St. Paul's words,

"Then we shall not be children any longer, tossed one way and another and carried along by every wind of doctrine, at the mercy of all the tricks men play and their cleverness in practicing deceit" (Eph. 4:14). But gradually seasoned by the values of Jesus Christ, we come into possession of trustworthy instincts. While still failing and, at times, still fooling ourselves, we can more habitually and more thoroughly trust our responses and intuitions. Thus matured, we become ready for that most important exercise of Christian stewardship: handing on to the next generation the practical wisdom of how Christians feel and act and believe.

**Christian Community and the Sense of the Faithful**

The transformation of our feelings into resources of seasoned and trustworthy instincts takes place in community. This suggests that the sensibilities of a faith community—like those of the individual believer—must mature into an internalized and dependable sense of faith. The challenge, as we have observed above, is to bring the traditional and rhetorical category of the sense of the faithful into dialogue with a specific community's religious maturing. Vatican II, with its reintroduction of this term into current Catholic theological discussion, authorizes us to attempt this dialogue.

In the *Constitution on the Church* issued at the Second Vatican Council, the sense of faith is understood as both universal and unerring:

> Thanks to a supernatural sense of the faith which characterizes the people as a whole, it manifests this unerring quality when, 'from the bishops down to the last member of the laity,' it shows universal agreement in matters of faith and morals.
> (*Lumen Gentium*, art. 12)

Both of these characteristics suggest a sense of faith that has little in common with the experience of an individual Christian community. This universal and unerring consensus about faith has usually been understood as a *received* sense: it is a sense that results from and remains fully dependent on the religious authority of the teaching Church.

Yet both in the Vatican II document and in the work of some theologians, a more active and generative aspect of this sense of faith can be discerned. In the *Constitution on the Church*, the sense of faith is further described by the use of three verbs:

> It *clings* without fail to the faith once delivered to the saints (Cf. Jude 3), *penetrates* it more deeply by accurate insights and *applies* it more thoroughly to life. (art. 12; our emphasis)

If the first verb suggests stability, the next two point to development and change. This may be not just a passive and docile sense that registers what the community has been taught, but an active and constructive sense of faith that grows and changes as a community applies its faith "more thoroughly to life."

This active aspect of the sense of faith and its location in specific communities were being explored well before Vatican II. J. P. Mackey, in *The Modern Theology of Tradition*, quotes the German theologian Scheeben on this sense of faith:

> The profession of faith by the body of believers is not of value only by reason of the influence of the Magisterium, which begets it, but possesses *its own intrinsic, relatively autonomous value* as a result of the direct working of the Holy Spirit on the faithful. (Mackey, p. 121; our emphasis)

This approach to the sense of the faithful brings it into contact with our discussion of a practical sense of faith: a specific community, like the individual Christian, comes to a sense of the faith that is intrinsic to it ("internalized" in our vocabulary), and that is relatively autonomous (as a trustworthy inner authority). Its source is the working of the Holy Spirit within this community of faith. Christian communities are not merely the passive recipients of faith (received from the hierarchical teaching Church), but are active generators of faith under the guidance of the Holy Spirit.

A century before Vatican II, Cardinal Newman turned to the notion of the sense of the faithful to argue for the importance of the laity in the preservation and growth of Christian faith. In a treatise entitled "On Consulting the Faithful in Matters of Doctrine," he stressed that the Christian faith abides first and most profoundly in specific communities; it does not exist in a prior and more thorough way in the hierarchy. (A prominent theologian of Newman's time was arguing the contrary, that revelation is given first to the hierarchy and only then mediated to individual communities of faith.) Indeed, Newman continued, the development of dogma (the elaboration of what we believe, such as in the Church's definition of the Trinity or the Assumption of Mary) comes from the official Church reflecting on a belief already long present in individual faith communities.

Newman, in listing the characteristics of this sense of the faithful, defined it "as a sort of instinct or *phronema*, deep in the bosom of the mystical body." *Phronema* is the noun form of *phronein* which we have already examined. Newman translates it as instinct, a bodily intuition shared by believers. Two of Newman's other characteristics offer additional insight into this collective sense. The sense of the faithful may be experienced "as an answer to its [a community's] prayers." This suggests a quite particular awareness, perhaps about a decision that needs to be made or a hoped-for resolution of a problem. What this understanding especially points to is both the concreteness of the awareness and its gradual development in the community. This would seem to be a sense of faith that is not a stable possession ("how we have always believed"), but a new insight in response to a new question in the Church. Contemporary examples might be new insights about the morality of artificial birth control, or the ordination of women, or the structural elements of social sin. Such senses would, expectably, arise gradually in some communities, both as an answer to their prayers and as a result of their seasoning in the faith. Only gradually would such "penetration and application" of faith come to be shared by the whole Church.

Newman's fifth characteristic of the sense of the faithful touches on inerrancy. Newman describes the sense of the faithful as "a jealousy of error, which it at once feels as a scandal." This characteristic points to the defensive function of the Church's instincts about its faith. Mature communities of faith guard against false feelings and unchristian instincts. It is the maturity of their seasoned sense of Christian faith that allows this community of the faithful to "at once feel" that a certain decision or development is false or wrong. To stay with Newman's image of a bodily instinct, the sense of the faithful allows this part of the body of Christ to sense foreign matter, to recognize the effects of harmful elements that may have gotten into the system. Such a seasoned instinct would recognize and reject both humanistic fads and fundamentalistic biases that attempt to pass as Christian insight.

A new and powerful interest in the sense of the faithful was in evidence at the international Synod of Catholic Bishops gathered in Rome in the Fall of 1980 for discussion of Christian family life. Cardinal Carter of Toronto questioned whether the experience of married Christians today might not be teaching the Church about the future shape of marriage. He asked if some of the new attitudes of mature Christians might be "a nonreflexive expression of the *sensus fidelium.*" By "nonreflexive" he meant a sense of the faithful concerning marriage that is not simply received from and reflective of the teaching Church, but may itself be generative of new insight. Cardinal Hume of Westminster, England, urged, in a similar vein, that the Church give greater attention to the marital experience of contemporary Christians: such experience, arising from the lives of seasoned Christians, is an important source (in his words, "a *fons theologica*") of the Church's sense of what Christian marriage should be.

At the end of the 1980 synod the participating bishops presented the Pope with forty-three resolutions about Christian marriage and the family. Three of the first four resolutions concerned the sense of faith in the Church. Resolution 2 pointed to the special relationship of this "appreciation of faith" (its translation of *sensus fidei*) to the life and witness of the laity. Resolution 3 conservatively repeated the traditional interpretation of this sense of faith: it entails universal agreement and "total conformity with the faith of all time and with all the faithful." Resolution 4 affirmed that the sense of faith "is the fruit of a living faith." It alluded to the growth of this sense and the development of "a way of life patterned on the beatitudes." While insisting that "the development of faith takes place only in the whole Church," this resolution did admit the practical origin of this sense: "It flows from those Christian families in which the sacrament of marriage is realized and revealed as an experience of faith." (We use here the English translation that appeared in the December 12, 1980 edition of the *National Catholic Reporter.*)

The official Church is today becoming more appreciative of what it has to learn from the lived faith of mature Christians. It has yet to fully appreciate that the sense of faith imbedded in maturing communities of faith is necessarily plural and divergent. Pluralism and differences within faith are still very frightening to many Church leaders. Dissent, debate, and divergence in faith—obvious and necessary aspects of the Church from its inception—continue to be denied and ignored. If we are to rescue the sense of the faithful from its (largely) rhetorical status, we must acknowledge its pluralistic nature and examine its role in the life of particular and different faith communities.

## Ministering to the Sense of the Faithful

The ministry to a community's sense of faith begins in the expectation that this group *has* such a sense. The maturing of a Christian community includes the development of a trustworthy instinct[3] of what its faith is and how, practically, it is to be lived. Such a sense of faith, as more than rhetorical, will express the individuality of this community as well as its oneness with the universal Church; it will bring this community both into a deeper unity and a livelier tension with the whole Church. Such a particularized sense of faith will also ground a community's identity and vocation. It helps the community come into a more profound sense of what it is for. Out of this sense of faith is born a community's generative ministry. Recognizing who we are and what our faith is for, we come to a sense of how we are to act. Our ministry—how we in this community of believers are to care for and challenge the world around us, in the name of Jesus Christ—takes its shape and direction from our practical sense of faith.

If the ministry to a community's sense of faith begins in the expectation that it have such an individualized awareness, this ministry proceeds as it forms and clarifies this sense of faith. Since it is a kind of collective conscience, this sense of faith always requires formation. The values of Jesus Christ and the gospels are brought again and again into this community's life—in its liturgies, its educational efforts, its practical decisions about money and other resources—and are allowed to shape its actions.

3. *"Sensus,"* as we have observed, has been translated in a great variety of ways. Our translation of "instinct," following Newman, is intended to counter the more cerebral translation of this sense as "a way of thinking." For some, "intuition" may be a less jarring and more suggestive translation than "instinct." The English translation of the resolutions of the 1980 Synod on the Family renders *sensus fidei* as an *"appreciation* of faith." This translation catches the more-than-rational savoring that *sensus* entails. Its only weakness may be a suggestion of passivity: in a "music appreciation course," for example, we learn to savor the sound, but do not play it ourselves. The sense of the faithful proper to a community of believers is an appreciation that leads to action: in the language of theology, it is a *sensus* that leads to *praxis*.

As this community's sense of faith matures over many years, it will need to be clarified repeatedly. Using the language of the *Constitution on the Church*, we will have to examine how this community is living out its faith; "clinging" to the faith of its tradition, "penetrating" this faith more deeply and accurately, and "applying" it more thoroughly to the changes in contemporary life.

This continual clarification will also teach a faith community about its role in the larger Church. As it reflects on its own faith, it clarifies the ways in which it is in accord and in conflict with the larger Church. Thus a community may come to certain convictions about justice that put it in conflict with an official Church position on the use of diocesan funds or with its position concerning the ordination of women. As this community examines these convictions, aware that its own insights are always in need of purification, it may also present these convictions as challenges to the diocese and other leadership groups in the Church. When communities can do this maturely—that is, with concreteness and patience and without personal attack or ultimatums—they perform a most important part of their own ministry. Such a ministry— that of a local community of faith to the larger Church—depends on a community's trust in its sense of faith. As with the individual conscience of a Christian, this collective conscience must not only be formed and purified, but also trusted. Maturity, for a community as well as for individuals, includes the ability to follow trustworthy instincts of faith.

The ministry of a community to the larger Church has become more prominent as we have clarified our understanding of Christian ministry itself. Ministry is less often seen today in a purely hierarchical context: ministry descending, in a one-directional fashion, from the Pope through the hierarchy to relatively passive communities of faith. In a Church again enlivened by its values of mutuality—our radical oneness in Jesus Christ which does away with ranks of status and prestige—we are recognizing the multi-directional quality of Christian ministry. As maturing Christians, we are all called to care for one another: every Christian is a "wounded healer"—called to heal others while acknowledging that he or she also stands in need of healing. If each individual Christian is both competent and wounded, graceful and sinful, this is also true of structures in our Church. Every part of our Church is grace-filled because God insists on dwelling here among us. And every part is also sinful because it is occupied and shaped by limited human beings as well.

What does this mean, practically, in a discussion of the sense of the faithful? It means that the infallible presence of God among us cannot be isolated in a single part of the Church. God's enduring presence belongs to the whole Church and so to every part, every genuine, maturing community of faith. Likewise, every part of the Church as sinful is in need of care and purification. That is, each community of faith has a ministry to other communities and to the larger Church itself. As it carefully clarifies its own sense of faith concerning specific aspects of Christian life (whether sexuality or celebration or social justice), a community can and must present the fruit of this reflection to the diocese and other leadership groups of the Church. These groups, themselves limited as is every part of the Church, await and depend on this ministry.

Such a ministry requires extraordinary maturity. A community—a parish, religious congregation, or diocese—must have the skills and patience to clarify and purify its own sense of faith. Then it must have the courage to present its conviction, aware of its fallibility, to the larger Church. A mature community will be able to withstand rejection: its tested sense of identity and vocation can survive conflict and disagreement. It is aware that new insights generated by particular communities will often be rejected by leadership groups in the Church—sometimes because they are wrong, sometimes because they are new.

Finally, some cautionary observations may be in order. We are reflecting here on something quite ordinary: a community's sense of purpose and conscience. But we are applying this ordinary aspect of group life to a traditional theological category and, in so doing, extending the category considerably. We are expanding the rhetorical aspect of a sense of the faithful to include the practical sense of faith and action of an individual community of faith. We are also assuming that the ideal of universal agreement, traditionally associated with this sense of faith, must be complemented by a greater awareness and appreciation of diversity. Pluriform and sometimes conflicting convictions about sexual expression, celebration, and involvement in social justice characterize Christian life today. As we argued in the first chapter of this book, this need not be interpreted only as a scandal. It can also be seen as a sign of the richness and variegation necessary in a universal and maturing Church. Most problematic, however, may be the active sense of community implied here. Can local communities of faith shake off centuries of passivity? Can parishes and other communities let go of long-familiar patterns of docility and acquiescence in which a restricted group of religious specialists (whether clergy, religious, or lay professional Church workers) ministered to and made religious decisions for a large group of childlike laity? The hope is that the movement of faith communities into their own religious maturity may be aided by this understanding of the sense of the faithful.

## FOR FURTHER REFLECTION

The sense of the faithful refers to the religious vitality of a community. To help this understanding become more concrete, consider a particular faith community that is important for you—a parish group, a ministry team, a religious congregation. Then reflect on these questions.

1. In what ways do members of this community experience a sense of belonging, of being included in the life of the group? How do members participate in the decisions and actions of this community?

2. In what areas of the community's life does it characteristically trust its own resources, have confidence in its own sense of direction? In what areas does it characteristically look "outside" for direction or approval?

3. What aspects of Christian life—worship, ministry, justice, sexuality, education, leadership—are being discussed or debated in the community now? How successful is the group in dealing with diversity? in moving toward consensus? Has the community been able to express a sense of its faith concerning one of these important questions?

## ADDITIONAL RESOURCES

Josef Rupert Geiselmann briefly traces some of the historical discussion of this sense in *The Meaning of Tradition* (Montreal: Palm, 1966). Geiselmann credits the nineteenth-century theologian Johann Möhler as being very influential in this history of this category. Möhler's understanding of this sense of faith as a kind of "tact" was translated in French as "instinct" and taken up in this form by Cardinal Newman.

Cardinal Newman's exploration of the sense of the faithful can be found in his *On Consulting the Faithful in Matters of Doctrine* (New York: Sheed & Ward, 1961). For a conservative interpretation of the sense of the faithful see James Hitchcock's "Thomas More and the Sensus Fidelium" in *The-*

*ological Studies* 36 (March 1975): 145–54. J. P. Mackey discusses this sense in his *The Modern Theology of Tradition* (New York: Herder & Herder, 1963).

Karl Rahner, in the 1965 edition of his *Theological Dictionary* (New York: Herder & Herder, p. 169), stresses the *instinctive* aspect of this sense of faith, as opposed to logical analysis. And although "the Magisterium indeed is its authentic interpreter, yet this Magisterium itself rests upon the faith of the whole Church, which is alive and can mature and grow in knowledge."

The importance of a refined sense of faith for any corporate reflection in the Church is emphasized in our *Method in Ministry* (New York: The Seabury Press, 1980): see especially pages 17–19 and 56–57.

Most practically, the rhetoric of a sense of the faithful is being clarified and tested in parish and diocesan councils. For a report on the disappointing results of post-Vatican II efforts to develop these forums of community reflection and decision-making, see Richard Schoenherr's and Eleanor Simpson's "The Political Economy of Diocesan Advisory Councils" (Madison, WI: Comparative Religious Organization Studies, 1978).

Perhaps the sense of faith resident in the body of believers can be related to Alcuin's assertion to Charlemagne in 800 that "the voice of the people is the voice of God *(vox populi vox Dei)*. Both phrases are extraordinarily ambiguous; they are also political in their suggestion of an authoritative grasp of the faith that is proper to a community.

For the full text of the *Constitution on the Church (Lumen Gentium)*, see Walter Abbott, Ed., *The Documents of Vatican II* (New York: America Press, 1966), pp. 14–96.

# Appendix:
# Additional References in the
# Sociology Of Community

A goal of this book has been to provide working knowledge about community. The intent of the several chapters in Part II has been to introduce those involved in the formation of the community of faith to the contemporary discussion of community in the social sciences, particularly in sociology.

Over recent years Christian ministers have become increasingly aware of the importance of the social sciences to their mission. There is among many religious persons today a greater appreciation of the ways in which the theoretical perspective of the social sciences influences contemporary culture. The empirical approach of the social sciences is recognized as a valuable starting point for understanding important aspects of human experience. More and more, church leaders use the research methods of the social sciences to investigate questions of vital concern. They turn to the findings of the social sciences for information to guide their choices in planning and action.

In light of this new awareness, a question emerges: How can the minister gain access to the methods and findings of the social sciences? We have taken up this question in our book *Method in Ministry*. The minister is not a professional social scientist. Thus, for the minister, as for most nonspecialists, some translation is necessary. What is needed is not a translation "down," as though to a less intelligent or less alert audience, but rather a translation "across," to an audience whose categories of thought and analysis are different, but not inferior.

In regard to the psychological sciences this translation is underway. There are sources to which the minister may turn for accurate and critical explanation of current psychological theory and practice. The movement of Clinical Pastoral Education has raised the level of psychological sophistication among many persons in ministry. Journals, such as *Pastoral Psychology, Religion and Health*, and *Journal of Pastoral Care*, have made psychological concepts, theory, and technique available to the reflective minister. University-based religious authors have made important contributions—Don Browning at the University of Chicago, Howard Clinebell at Claremont, Eugene Kennedy at Loyola University in Chicago, James Lapsley at Princeton, Henri Nouwen at Yale, and others. As a result of these and other efforts, many religious people today feel at home in psychology. They can draw upon and use appropriately its categories and approaches to illumine their pastoral understanding and to guide their pastoral practice. They are sufficiently critical to know the difference between psychology and religion and can bring the two perspectives into creative tension.

However, this is not the case in regard to sociology. The work of Peter Berger, Joseph Fichter, and Andrew Greeley has brought sociology to the attention of some in ministry. But generally, there is much less familiarity with the concepts and approaches that guide sociological analysis, much less awareness of the connections between sociological findings and ministry, much less sense that there is anything of value here to be learned. The appearance of Gregory Baum's important work *Religion and Alienation* marks a significant step toward the remedy of this lack. Baum designates his effort "a theological reading of sociology." In it his goal is to "make use of sociological concepts and insights to understand more clearly what Christian practice should be in the present and how we can more adequately formulate the presence of the Holy Spirit in society." The efforts of critical theology in Germany and liberation theology in Latin America and other areas of the Third World (both influenced by Marxian analysis) offer additional examples of the dialogue between sociological analysis and theological interpretation. The discussion of community in which we are engaged in this volume is another effort to use sociology's concepts and insights, both to support and to challenge Christian practice.

The sociological literature on community is a rich resource, one that should be accessible not only to the sociologically trained expert in the Church but to the reflective believer and minister as well. This book has attempted to make more widely available an understanding of community that is derived from the sociological tradition and that can be of value within the believing community. Its intent has been not to give answers but access—to invite religious persons into conversation with the categories and concepts of sociology's understanding of community. This Appendix offers an annotated bibliography which may serve as a guide for those who wish to go further in this conversation.

"Aspects of Community." *American Journal of Sociology* 82 (1976):291–355. The entire September 1976 issue of this prestigious journal is devoted to reports from a symposium representing the current "state of the art" in the sociology of community.

Back, Kurt W. *In Search of Community: Encounter Group and Social Change*. Washington, D.C.: American Association for the Advancement of Science, 1978. This book makes available a number of provocative papers originally presented in a seminar directed to the analysis of the encounter group movement in the United States through the 1960s and 70s. Several papers discuss the cultural factors that fuel the search for community among certain groups in American life.

Bernard, Jesse. *The Sociology of Community*. Glenview, Il.: Scott, Foresman Co., 1973. An eminent contemporary sociologist, Bernard provides a useful discussion and critique of what she judges to be the "four classical paradigms [that] encompass most of what we know about the sociology of the community."

Bott, Elizabeth, *Family and Social Network*. Second edition. New York: Free Press, 1972. Bott gives evidence of the current shape of personal allegiance and interaction which calls into question the images of the nuclear family unit and geographically enclosed neighborhood.

Effrat, Marcia Pelly. "Approaches to Community." In her *The Community: Approaches and Applications*. New York: Free Press, 1974, pp. 1–32. A valuable overview, Effrat's chapter offers examples of four major research traditions through which sociologists are attempting to describe community.

Goode, William J. "Community within a Community: The Professions." In David W. Minar and Scott Greer, eds. *The Concept of Community: Readings with Interpretations*. Chicago: Aldine Publishing Co., 1969, pp. 152–62. Starting from the premise that "each profession is a community without physical locus," Goode explores the notion of the "functional community" based on common values and interests. Other selections in this collection of papers may also be of interest to a beginning reader in the sociological discussion of community.

Gottlieb, Benjamin H., ed. *Social Networks and Social Support*. New York: Sage Publications, 1981. In a series of essays, scholars and human services practitioners explore the current shape of the natural networks of human attachment—family ties, mutual help groups, voluntary associations—and their function in contemporary social experience.

Gusfield, Joseph R. *Community: A Critical Response*. Oxford: Basil Blackwell, 1975. In this excellent analysis of the state of current sociological theory concerning community, Gusfield distinguishes the "territorial" from the "relational" meaning of this term. He goes on to examine the special significance of the concept of community for the analysis of social change.

Kraus, William A. *Collaboration in Organizations: Alternatives to Hierarchy*. New York: Human Sciences Press, 1980. The field of organization development has contributed effectively toward the resolution of practical questions of group life. In this book Kraus challenges some central concepts and strategies of this burgeoning discipline, urging a review of the central values of competition and hierarchy that underlie much individual behavior and group structure in the West.

*Robert MacIver on Community, Society, and Power*. Edited by Leon Bramson. Chicago: University of Chicago Press, 1970. This is a collection of the work of an early and influential American sociologist of community.

McWilliams, Wilson Carey. *The Idea of Fraternity in America*. Berkeley: University of California Press, 1974. A historian of ideas, McWilliams traces the development and expression of the ideal of civic "brotherhood" from the founding documents of the American democracy into the 20th century.

Misra, Bhabagrahi and James Preston, eds. *Community, Self and Identity*. Chicago: Aldine Publishing Co., 1978. The papers in this collection examine the new "intentional" communities from an anthropological perspective, sensitive to similarities and differences between these groups and other more traditional "natural" human communities. There is special consideration given to the importance of the religious element in group life.

Nisbet, Robert. "Community," in his *The Sociological Tradition*. New York: Basic Books, 1966, pp. 47–106. Nisbet traces the use of *community* as a sociological category in the work of important nineteenth-century founders of the discipline: Ferdinand Tönnies, Frederic LePlay, Karl Marx, Max Weber, Emile Durkheim, Georg Simmel.

Scherer, Jacqueline. *Contemporary Community: Sociological Illusion or Reality?* New York: Harper & Row, 1973. Scherer draws upon the evidence of contemporary research to explore the experience of community in the structures of modern life. She includes a chapter on the parish.

Schmalenbach, Herman. "The Sociological Category of Communion." In Talcott Parsons *et al. Theories of Society*, vol. 1. New York: Free Press, 1961. A classic in the German tradition of sociological analysis, this paper draws one of the early distinctions between form and feeling in regard to community.

Sennett, Richard, *The Uses of Disorder: Personal Identity and City Life.* New York: Vintage Books, 1970. Sennett challenges the nostalgic critique of city life as hostile to human and social development. There are clear implications here regarding realistic goals for community in the religious context. See also his *The Fall of Public Man* (New York: Vintage Books, 1978) and *Authority* (New York: Vintage Books, 1981).

Stein, Maurice. *The Eclipse of Community.* Princeton, N.J.: Princeton University Press, 1972. Stein discusses what has been learned about the structure of community life from the tradition of community studies in American sociology. His interpretive chapters in Part III are particularly valuable.

Turner, Victor. *The Ritual Process.* Ithaca, N.Y.: Cornell University Press, 1969. See also his "Passages, Margins, and Poverty: Religious Symbols of Communitas." *Worship 42* (1972): 390–412 and 482–494. An anthropologist, Turner makes an important contribution to an understanding of the function of the psychological experience of community (his *communitas*) to the structure and vitality of group life.

# Bibliography

Abbott, Walter M., ed., *The Documents of Vatican II*. New York: America Press, 1966.

Arendt, Hannah. *The Human Condition*. Chicago: University of Chicago Press, 1958.

Ash, James. "The Decline of Ecstatic Prophecy in the Early Church." *Theological Studies* 37 (1976): 227–52.

"Aspects of Community." *American Journal of Sociology* 82 (1976): 291–355.

Augsberger, David. *Caring Enough to Confront*. Scottsdale, PA: Herald Press, 1980.

Back, Kurt W. *In Search of Community: Encounter Group and Social Change*. Washington, D.C.: American Association for the Advancement of Science, 1978.

Banks, Robert. *Paul's Idea of Community*. Grand Rapids, MI: Wm. B. Eerdmans Publishing Co., 1980.

Berger, Peter, and Richard Neuhaus. *To Empower People*. Washington, D.C.: American Enterprise Institute, 1977.

Bernard, Jesse. *The Sociology of Community*. Glenview, IL: Scott, Foresman, 1973.

Bonhoeffer, Dietrich. *Life Together*. New York: Harper & Row, 1976.

Bott, Elizabeth. *Family and Social Network*. second edition. New York: Free Press, 1972.

Bradford, Leland P. *Group Development*. San Diego, CA: University Associates, 1978.

Braxton, Edward. *The Wisdom Community*. New York: Paulist Press, 1980.

Brown, Raymond. *The Community of the Beloved Disciple*. New York: Paulist Press, 1979.

———. *Crises Facing the Chruch*. New York: Paulist Press, 1975.

———. "Other Sheep in the Fold: The Johannine Perspective on Christian Diversity in the Late First Century." *Journal of Biblical Literature* 97 (1978): 5–22.

Brill, Naomi I. *Teamwork: Working Together in the Human Services*. New York: Lippincott, 1976.

Buckley, Michael J. "Mission in Companionship." *Studies in the Spirituality of Jesuits* 11, no. 4 (1979): 1–46.

Champlin, Joseph M. *The Living Parish*. Notre Dame, IN: Ave Maria Press, 1977.

"The Church as Communion." *Jurist* 35 (1976): 4–245.

"Community and Privacy." *Humanitas* 11 (1975): 5–113.

Cooke, Bernard. *Ministry to Word and Sacraments.* Philadelphia: Fortress Press, 1975.

"Cultures and Communities." *Lumen Vitae* 32 (1977): 143–277.

Delepesse, Max. *The Church Community: Leaven and Life-Style.* Notre Dame, IN: Ave Maria Press, 1973.

Dittes, Joseph E. *When the People Say No: Conflict and the Call to Ministry.* San Francisco: Harper & Row, 1979.

Dobbelaere, K., and J. Billiet. "Community-Formation and the Church." In M. Caudron, ed., *Faith and Society*, pp. 211–59. Louvain: University of Louvain, 1978.

Donnelly, Dody. *Team.* New York: Paulist Press, 1979.

Effrat, Marcia Pelly. *The Community: Approaches and Application.* New York: Free Press, 1974.

Egan, Gerard. *Interpersonal Living.* Monterey, CA: Brooks/Cole, 1976.

———. *The Skilled Helper.* second edition. Monterey, CA: Brooks/Cole, 1981.

———. *Systematic Helping.* Monterey, CA: Brooks/Cole, 1982.

———. *You and Me: The Skills of Communicating and Relating to Others.* Monterey, CA: Brooks/Cole, 1977.

———, and Michael Cowan. *People in Systems.* Monterey, CA: Brooks/Cole, 1979.

Emmons, Michael, and David Richardson. *The Assertive Christian.* Minneapolis: Winston Press, 1980.

Erikson, Erik. *Childhood and Society.* second edition. New York: W.W. Norton & Co., 1963.

———. *Identity: Youth and Crisis.* New York: W.W. Norton & Co., 1968.

Fagan, Harry. *Empowerment: Skills for Parish Social Action.* New York: Paulist Press, 1979.

Fenhagen, James. *Mutual Ministry.* New York: The Seabury Press, 1977.

Fleming, David. "Community, Corporateness, and Communion." In Lora Ann Quiñonez, ed., *Starting Points*, pp. 33–44. Washington, D.C.: Leadership Conference of Women Religious, 1980.

Fowler, James. *Stages of Faith.* New York: Harper & Row, 1981.

Geiselmann, Josef Rupert. *The Meaning of Tradition.* Montreal: Palm, 1966.

Goode, William J. "Community within a Community: The Professions." In David W. Minar and Scott Greer, eds., *The Concept of Community: Readings with Interpretations*, pp. 152–62. Chicago: Aldine Publishing Co., 1969.

Gordon, William, and Roger Howe. *Team Dynamics in Developing Organizations.* Dubuque: Kendall/Hunt, 1977.

Gottlieb, Benjamin H., ed. *Social Networks and Social Support.* New York: Sage Publications, 1981.

Greeley, Andrew, ed. *The Family in Crisis or in Transition.* New York: The Seabury Press, 1979.

Gusfield, Joseph R. *Community: A Critical Response.* Oxford: Basil Blackwell, 1975.

Hammet, Rosine, and Loughlin Sofield. *Inside Christian Community.* New York: Levacq Publishing, 1981.

Haroutunian, Joseph. *God with Us: A Theology of Transpersonal Life.* Philadelphia: Westminster Press, 1980.

Hart, Thomas N. *The Art of Christian Listening.* New York: Paulist Press, 1981.

Haughton, Rosemary. *The Transformation of Man.* Revised Edition. Springfield, IL: Templegate, 1980.

Henriot, P. J., J. A. Appleyard, and J. L. Klein. "Living Together in Mission." *Studies in the Spirituality of Jesuits* 12, no. 2 (1980): 1–37.

Hitchcock, James. "Thomas More and the Sensus Fidelium." *Theological Studies* 36 (1975): 145–54.

Inter-Religious Task Force for Social Analysis. *Must We Choose Sides? Christian Commitment for the 1980s.* New York: Episcopal Church Publishing, 1979.

Janeway, Elizabeth. *The Powers of the Weak.* New York: Alfred A. Knopf, 1980.

Kaesemann, Ernst. *Commentary on Romans.* Grand Rapids, MI: Wm. B. Eerdmans Publishing Co., 1980.

———. *Essays on New Testament Themes.* Naperville, IL: Allenson, 1964.

Kanter, Rosebeth Moss. *Commitment and Community.* Cambridge, MA: Harvard University Press, 1972.

Keating, Charles. *Community: Learning to Live in Diocesan, Religious and Parish Communities.* St. Meinrad, IN: Abbey Press, 1977.

———. *The Pastoral Planning Book.* New York: Paulist Press, 1981.

Kirschenbaum, Howard, and Barbara Glaser. *Developing Support Groups.* San Diego, CA: University Associates, 1978.

Koester, Helmut. "*Gnomai Diaphoroi:* The Origins and Nature of Diversification in the History of Early Christianity." *Harvard Theological Review* 58 (1965): 279–318.

Kraus, William A. *Collaboration in Organizations: Alternatives to Hierarchy.* New York: Human Sciences Press, 1980.

Lacoursiere, Roy. *The Life Cycle of Groups.* New York: Human Sciences Press, 1980.

Leas, Speed B. *A Lay Person's Guide to Conflict Management.* Washington, D.C.: Alban Institute, 1981.

Lee, Dorothy. *Valuing the Self.* Englewood Cliffs, NJ: Prentice-Hall, 1976.

LeVerdiere, Eugene, and William Thompson. "New Testament Communities." In Wm. Thompson and Walter Burghardt, eds., *Why the Church?*, pp. 22–34. New York: Paulist Press, 197?.

Levinson, Daniel. *The Seasons of a Man's Life.* New York: Alfred A. Knopf, 1978.

*Life Together: A Study of Religious Association.* Lockport, IL: Christian Brothers' National Office, 1978.

MacIver, Robert. *On Community Society, and Power.* Edited by Leon Bramson. Chicago: University of Chicago Press, 1970.

Mackey, J. P. *The Modern Theology of Tradition.* New York: Herder & Herder, 1963.

McKinley, John. *Group Development through Participant Training.* New York: Paulist Press, 1980.

McWilliams, Wilson Carey. *The Idea of Fraternity in America.* Berkeley: University of California Press, 1974.

Metz, Johann Baptist. *The Emergent Church.* New York: Crossroad Publishing Co., 1981.

Miller, John M. *The Contentious Community: Constructive Conflict in the Church.* Philadelphia: Westminster Press, 1978.
Misra, Bhabagrahi, and James Preston, eds. *Community, Self and Identity.* Chicago: Aldine Publishing Co., 1978.
Mohler, James. *The Origin and Evolution of the Priesthood.* New York: Alba House, 1970.
Moloney, Francis J. *Disciples and Prophets: A Biblical Model for the Religious Life.* New York: Crossroad Publishing Co., 1981.
"New Forms of Community." *IDOC-International*, North American Edition. (March 25, 1972): 2–70.
Newman, John. *On Consulting the Faithful in Matters of Doctrine.* New York: Sheed and Ward, 1961.
Nisbet, Robert. *The Sociological Tradition.* New York: Basic Books, 1966.
Nouwen, Henri. *Clowning in Rome.* New York: Doubleday & Co., 1979.
Palmer, Parker. *The Company of Strangers: Christians and the Renewal of Public Life.* New York: Crossroad Publishing Co., 1981.
———. *Going Public.* Washington, D.C.: Alban Institute, 1980.
Pelikan, Jaroslav. "Theology and Change." *Crosscurrents* 19 (1969): 375–84.
Perrin, Norman. *Jesus and the Language of the Kingdom.* Philadelphia: Fortress Press, 1976.
*Power and Authority.* Lockport, IL: Christian Brothers' National Office, 1975.
Rademacher, William J. *The Practical Guide for Parish Councils.* Mystic, CT: Twenty-third Publications, 1980.
Rahner, Karl. *Concern for the Church. Theological Investigations XX.* New York: Crossroad Publishing Co., 1981.
———, and others. *Theological Dictionary.* New York: Herder & Herder, 1965.
Roy, Paul L. *Building Christian Communities for Justice.* New York: Paulist Press, 1981.
Russell, Letty. *The Future of Partnership.* Philadelphia: Westminster Press, 1979.
Sarason, Seymour. *The Psychological Sense of Community.* San Francisco: Jossey-Bass, 1974.
Scherer, Jacqueline. *Contemporary Community: Sociological Illusion or Reality?* New York: Harper & Row, 1973.
Schillebeeckx, Edward. *Jesus: An Experiment in Christology.* New York: Crossroad Publishing Co., 1979.
———. *Ministry: Leadership in the Community of Jesus Christ.* New York: Crossroad Publishing Co., 1980.
Schmalenbach, Herman. "The Sociological Category of Communion." In Talcott Parsons et al., *Theories of Society*, volume 1, pp. 1067–77. New York: Free Press, 1961.
Schnackenburg, Rudolf. *God's Rule and Kingdom.* New York: Herder & Herder, 1963.
Schoenherr, Richard A., and Eleanor P. Simpson. *The Political Economy of Diocesan Advisory Councils.* Madison, WI: Comparative Religious Organization Studies, 1978.
Segundo, Juan Luis. *The Community Called Church.* Maryknoll, NY: Orbis Books, 1973.
Sennett, Richard. *Authority.* New York: Vintage Books, 1981.

————. *The Fall of Public Man*. New York: Vintage Books, 1978.
————. *The Uses of Disorder: Personal Identity and City Life*. New York: Vintage Books, 1970.
Shea, John. "A Theological Perspective on Human Relations Skills and Family Intimacy." In Andrew Greeley, ed., *The Family in Crisis or in Transition*, pp. 89–99. New York: The Seabury Press, 1979.
Silverman, Phyliss. *Mutual Help Groups: Organization and Development*. New York: Sage Publications, 1980.
Slater, Philip. *The Pursuit of Loneliness*. Boston: Beacon Press, 1970.
Sobrino, Jon. *Christology at the Crossroads*. New York: Orbis Books, 1978.
Stein, Maurice. *The Eclipse of Community*. Expanded Edition. Princeton, NJ: Princeton University Press, 1972.
Thompson, William. "Conflict, Anger and Growth in the Church." *Chicago Studies* 12 (1973): 39–46.
Tracy, David. "The Catholic Model of Caritas: Self-transcendence and Transformation." In Andrew Greeley, ed., *The Family in Crisis or in Transition*, pp. 100–10. New York: The Seabury Press, 1979.
Turner, Victor. "Passages, Margins, and Poverty: Religious Symbols of Communitas." *Worship* 46 (1972): 390–412, 482–94.
————. *The Ritual Process*. Ithaca, NY: Cornell University Press, 1969.
Vanier, Jean. *Community and Growth: Our Pilgrimage Together*. New York: Paulist Press, 1979.
Whitehead, Evelyn Eaton, ed. *The Parish in Community and Ministry*. New York: Paulist Press, 1978.
————, and James D. Whitehead. *Christian Life Patterns*. New York: Doubleday & Co., 1979.
Whitehead, James D., and Evelyn Eaton Whitehead. *Method in Ministry: Theological Reflection and Christian Ministry*. New York: The Seabury Press, 1980.
————. *Marrying Well: Possibilities in Christian Marriage Today*. New York: Doubleday & Co., 1981.
Wilken, Robert. *The Myth of Christian Beginnings*. Notre Dame, IN: University of Notre Dame Press, 1980.

# Name & Subject Index

## NOTES ON THE AUTHORS

*Evelyn Eaton Whitehead* is a developmental and social psychologist, with a doctorate from the University of Chicago. She writes and lectures on questions of adult development, aging, and the analysis of community as a style of group life. *James D. Whitehead* is a pastoral theologian and historian of religion. He holds the doctorate from Harvard University, with a concentration in Chinese religions. His professional interests include issues of contemporary spirituality and theological method in ministry.

The Whiteheads are authors of *Method in Ministry*, published by Seabury Press in 1980. In addition, they have written *Marrying Well: Possibilities in Christian Marriage Today* and *Christian Life Patterns*, which was chosen as a selection of the Catholic Book Club. They are frequent contributors to professional and pastoral journals.

In 1978 they established Whitehead Associates, through which they serve as consultants in education and ministry. They are members of the associate faculty of the Institute of Pastoral Studies at Loyola University in Chicago.